ABOUT THE AUTHOR

Fellow of the Royal Historical Society and of the Society for Advanced Legal Studies of the University of London, Dr. MARK A. SAMMUT SASSI, (b. 1973), has studied law, diplomatic studies, and translation studies at the University of Malta, legal theory and legal history at the University of London, historical sociology at the London School of Economics, international politics at the University of Leicester, and historical studies at Oxford University. He is a member of the European Society for Comparative Legal History, the European Society for History of Law, the Società italiana di storia del diritto, and the Malta Historical Society. He has written a number of books on law, history, and politics, published in Malta and the UK. His publications include: *L-Istorja tal-Latvja fil-Qosor/A Short History of Latvia*, Malta: 2004; *Il-Liġi, il-Morali, u r-Raġuni* (with Giuseppe Mifsud Bonnici), Malta: 2008; *The Mediterranean: Different Perspectives, Common Objectives* (co-author), Italy: 2010; *Malta at the European Court of Human Rights 1987-2012* (editor and co-author), Malta: 2012; *Essays in Maltese Legal History and Comparative Law Volume 1*, UK: 2017; "Civil Law" in *Elgar Encyclopedia of Crime and Criminal Justice* (with Aniceto Masferrer) (Pedro Caeiro, Sabine Gless, Valsamis Mitsilegas, Miguel João Costa, Janneke De Snaijer, and Georgia Theodorakakou, eds.), UK: 2024.

Painting on the cover:

Vers l'Ouest (1955)
by Arpad Szenes
(Budapest, 1897–Paris, 1985),
Musée des Beaux-Arts,
Dijon, France.

Printed in the United Kingdom.

ISBN: 978-1-912142-45-3

Essays in Maltese Legal History Vol. 2

Mark A.
Sammut Sassi

Essays in Maltese Legal History

Volume 2

P3rtınənt Press

Contents

Almost a Preface

Giovanni Bonello

When Mark A. Sammut is holding your hand, you find yourself levitating towards the higher rungs of the philosophy of law and of history of legislation. So far, Malta has had some honest, even diligent, recorders of facts, but we were missing the thinkers who made those factoids meaningful. All law, not less criminal and constitutional law, subsists on many different levels. Other scholars help you scratch the surface. Sammut mines for gold far deeper into the bowels of knowledge and of reasoning. He places history at the service of legislation, and law as a major architect of history.

The hefty essays that make up this book end up being necessary updates to our meagre histories of legislation, bedevilled by adversities on all sides. Not unlike political chronicle, the intricacies of our centuries of law-building have often been deodorized by pro-colonial historians. Sammut is no stooge who feels compelled to feed the masses those doctored fables their owners would love them to believe. He acknowledges only one master – the quest for truth. Like me, the author may question whether in history there are ultimate truths– but he never doubts the existence of ultimate falsehoods. The first we cannot always guarantee, the second we must always repulse.

Perusing these pages, I am left stunned by the fastidious perseverance of Mark Sammut. Aficionados of Maltese legal history had probably heard of Sir John Joseph Dillon, but never before had his 1807 intellectual cogitations on the juridical sequences and origin of British Malta been examined so thoroughly and competently. More importantly, have they been contextualized with their philosophical roots, their political undertones, their cultural baggage and their power imperatives. What a revelation!

And the writings of Amabile Bonello, an almost entirely unknown patriot whose case for Malta's legal right to self-government, if not self-determination, that compulsive journalist had already advocated coherently a hundred years before independence. Bonello pleaded with passion, scholarship and courage, almost scandalous and seditious for his times, in a nation comatose to the calls of nationalism then raging all over the rest of continental Europe.

The year 1848 saw popular uprisings in virtually every European nation then under the yolk of another nation. Shamefully, Malta distinguished itself by being about the only subjected country in the whole of Europe where colonial servility proclaimed business as usual. The inhabitants just did not care – some whimpers of protest, but not one faint rumble of popular turmoil.

Coincidentally, my own birth year falls on the centenary of Amabile Bonello's. I have no idea whether we share any DNA, though I do not believe I would be mortified if we did. He remains one of the very few to have learnt something from 1848, who found the mettle to give a voice to national dignity. He died tragically in 1879, drowning at sea. More tragically still, the colonial stooges made sure to drown him a second time in the national memory. No portrait of his seems to have survived.

Apart from some references in Bianca Fiorentini's history of journalism, as far as I could ascertain Sammut's paper remains the first and only monument to Bonello's contribution to building the foundations of our nationhood and of our constitutional edifice. Rightfully, his place in 19th century history should not be behind that of Vassalli, Brared, Bres, Mitrovich, Sceberras and Fortunato Mizzi.

This collection also showcases some seminal essays of the evolution of criminal doctrine in Malta. I know that Dr Sammut has some very focussed views on the influence Cesare Beccaria exerted on the evolution of penal law in Europe and, tangentially, in Malta. My personal inspiration homes on a lesser-known compatriot of Beccaria, imported into the island by a naïve Grand Master to reform the laws, the courts and the legal professions. Giandonato Rogadeo in 1781 tried his utmost to do that. He came, he saw, and he threw up. His voluminous observations would be fertile pastures for Dr Sammut to graze in.

Our islands repeatedly found themselvesat the crossroads of history, the point where different, sometimes conflicting, legal cultures tried to coalesce and intermarry - the British common law, with continental statutory law, the inquisitorial and the accusatorial system in criminal matters, a rigid over a flexible constitution, the doctrine of binding precedent as opposed to the rationales of philosophy of law, the supremacy of parliament pitted against the supremacy of the constitution.

Since the beginning of the British connection when this miscegenation started in earnest, our legislators seem to have striven to enjoy the best of both worlds. Not infrequently, they ended with the worse of either.

Dr Sammut has demonstrated a particularly rare genius at unravelling how and when the various rivers of thought flowing in different, sometimes opposite directions, at some point met and energised each other.

Welcome to these challenging and unsuspected discoveries.

23 March 2024

Introduction

There is a big and not inconsequential difference between history of legislation and legal history (or history of law). I would argue that history of legislation is but one of the many constituent elements of legal history.

Most if not all Maltese advocates who do litigation are, in a sense, historians of legislation. It is usual for such advocates to look up the legislative itinerary of norms from the moment they are conceived by a politician or a lobbyist, onward till the moment they are signed into law, through their progress along the production chain – drafting, public consultation, readings in Parliament. At every stage of the law-making ritual, there are hints which the shrewd advocate catches and then makes use of to prove or disprove one or more points. The Court, it is assumed, is there to carry out the will of the legislator (the representative of the People), and that will can only be established once the legislator's intentions are extracted from the primary sources: mostly, but not exclusively, parliamentary debates.

None of the essays in this colletion purports to do anything of the sort. One day, I might write a monograph about one particular Chapter of the Laws of Malta, treating the subject from a purely history-of-legislation point of view. But this is not what I have done in these essays.

These essays are essays on history of law. It is true that identifying the intention of the legislator is, in perhaps more senses than one, an exercise in social history. But legal history *per se* is more straightforwardly social, understood in the widest sense possible: philosophy, sociology, politics, and so on.

My interest is mostly piqued by the history of ideas. Ideas are shaped by intergroup conflicts, politics, philosophy, and economics. Ideology is indeed the distillate of these social phenomena. According to certain authors, legal history can fall between two stools: law and history; however, I see it as another facet of history, possibly the most important, since human social behaviour is regulated and often determined by the law.

In the essays collected here, I focus on constitutional and criminal law. These two laws in Malta follow the flow created by philosophy, politics, and economics. The history of Maltese nineteenth-century law is interesting because it is the story of an Italo-French(ified) elite class trying to accommodate the polite yet strict expectations of the new, very alien masters without losing its soul. Until 1798, the elites of Malta were used to the pan-European, Catholic Knights most of whom still perceived international politics in terms of Christendom and feudalism, not of imperialism as the fuel of the new, liberal economy. From 1800 onward, following the two-year Revolutionary interruption, the Maltese elites had to bow their heads before a maritime power that had just lost a huge New World empire and was uncertain of its future role in the world but was about to embark, in the most *laissez-faire* way imaginable, on the creation of a new, even bigger Old World empire that was to cover something between one-sixth and one-fifth of the planet's surface. These new masters embraced a *sui-generis* conception of Christianity, that seriously believed that theirs was the true Reformed Catholic (i.e., "all-embracing") Church, immune to the moral corruption of Popism and free of the idolatry of the Romish Church. Their monarch was the "Defender of the Faith", and their kingdom blessed with "Israelism" (as expounded in J.H. Allen's 1902 *Judah's Sceptre and Joseph's Birthright*). Empire would allow them to convert the heathen to Christianity and to proselytise for English devotion to hard work, moral probity, sexual restraint, scientific method, business acumen, and legal practicality. These were the new masters the Italo-French(ified) elites of Malta had to say "Yes sir!" to. Unlike the African kings and chieftains, the Maltese did not need gunboat diplomacy to grasp the increasingly obvious fact that from the 1830s onward, Britain would occupy for many decades – possibly even forever, as the sun did not seem inclined to set on the Empire – the number-one position in the world. But whatever the impression they gave, the highly-civilised Italo-French(ified) elites of Malta were not ready to kow-tow so easily to the new masters. The elites of Malta expected protection in exchange of fealty, not occuption leading to a front-line role in the furtherance of imperial interests. The Maltese were still caught in the old, Christendom-feudalism worldview espoused by the Knights; the British worldview was new: liberalism-imperialism.[1]

In Malta, the economy was imperial, not "national". Local enterprise was not a priority for the foreign masters, given that it was in the interests of the Empire to keep the colony always in need to suckle at the breast of the mother country. Allowing the colony to attain self-sufficiency would allow

---

1 See Domenico Losurdo (2005/2011), *Liberalism: A Counter-History* (Gregory Elliott, tr.), London: Verso.

the colony eventually to leave the mother country and face the world all by herself. Like a narcissistic mother, the mother country had to treat the daughter colony as an extension not as a separate entity, and to clip its wings constantly lest it fly away from the nest. The mother country had to convince the daughter colony that without the warm embrace of the imperial family, the colony would be doomed, as the colony did not have the adequate level of civilisation to be accepted in the fold of the other family, that of civilised nations.[2] The mother country convinced the daughter colony that it had still to attain the level of civilisation that would enable it to appreciate English law and liberty, and to put into practice the economic acumen of the English nation. Only these qualities would allow the daughter colony to make it by herself in the lawless, harsh world of international affairs.

The foreign master discouraged local colonial industry, petrifying the colonial economy to accept its destiny as utensil for the Empire. The economy was colonial and the legal framework imperial. Within these two constraints many of the laws of Malta were forged, but also many of the constituent elements of the Maltese mentality. These essays are an attempt to challenge the mentality bequeathed to a small, insular community by a huge, world-wide empire for the benefit of the mightier of the two.

For the moment, my interest lies mostly in the early- to mid-nineteenth century. Further on, I aim to expand my areas of interest to analyse the latter half of the eighteenth century, in the context of the *long* nineteenth century. Much of my time will be devoted to Giandonato Rogadeo and the cultural world he sprang from and interacted with. There was indeed a Neapolitan Enlightenment, dominated by Vico, Filangieri, Genovese, and others. Right now, I'm writing about a Sicilian jurist who inhabited that world. Once that's done, it will be the turn of the *dramatis personae* of the eighteenth century. It's neither a promise nor a threat... but a little note to my future self.

My heartfelt thanks goes to Giovanni Bonello for accepting to write this book's Preface and for his constant encouragement. I owe him a great debt of gratitude that words can only defectively convey.

20 March 2024
Vernal Equinox
World Storytelling Day

---

2 The Latin Americans faced this uphill struggle upon attaining independence in the nineteenth century, because of their *mestizo* and *mulatto* populations.

CRIMINAL LAW

An Enlightened Shadow? Elements of the Intellectual Climate at the Time of the Codification of the Criminal Law of Malta

Appeared in *Comparative Legal History*, 9 (2021) 2

Introduction

For legal history, the late eighteenth and early nineteenth centuries are a transition period, when one epoch ended and a new one (the contemporary) began.[1] The Criminal Code of Malta was drafted in this period marked by the revolutions in North America (1776) and France (1789) and the new political infrastructure they brought in their wake – which can be termed 'liberal' or 'constitutional' – and that, in turn, transformed or renewed the law.[2] For certain scholars, this transformation was a rupture with the existing system; others believe it was not. It is a period that is complex to understand and describe, for the entire West but more so for Malta. Western Europe was going through an epochal change; Malta was going through that change while concurrently experiencing the encounter of two European legal traditions (the accusatorial and the inquisitorial) on its small territory. The epochal change had something to do with widespread nascent nationalism, which, in Malta, was stunted because of its territorial size.

This article will attempt to give a preliminary overview of the changes occurring in the criminal laws of the Italian-speaking part of Europe, which is the world that the Maltese followed at the time, and the peculiar experience of Malta during the historical moment when the accusatorial and inquisitorial systems met.

I am grateful to Professor Victor Mallia-Milanes of the University of Malta and to former European Court of Human Rights Judge Giovanni Bonello for reading and commenting on a previous version of this article. I am likewise indebted to Michael Schiavone (2009), co-editor of the *Dictionary of Maltese Biographies*, Malta: PIN, for his invaluable assistance in the research on Maltese students at the University of Pisa in the early nineteenth century. Finally, I thank the two anonymous reviewers for their comments. All errors are, however, my own.

1 Thomas Vormbaum and Michael Bohlander (2014), *A Modern History of German Criminal Law* (Berlin: Springer-Verlag) 18. See also Jean-Marie Carbasse (1990), *Introduction historique au droit penal,* Paris: PUF, 301–14; *idem* (1994), 'État autoritaire et justice répressive. L'évolution de la législation penale de 1789 au Code Pénal de 1810' in *All'Ombra dell'Aquila Imperiale. Trasformazioni e continuità istituzionali nei territori sabaudi in età napoleonica (1802-1814). Atti del Convegno, Torino 15-18 ottobre 1990,* Vol I, Ministero per i beni culturali e ambientali, 314.

2 Aniceto Masferrer (2016), 'Codification as Nationalisation or Denationalisation of Law: The Spanish Case in Comparative Perspective' (2016) 4 *Comparative Legal History* 104.

The law in Malta before the Criminal Code

The Municipal Code of 1784,[3] which preceded the Criminal Code of 1854 and contained the statute element of the criminal laws of Malta, existed in a jurisprudential legal system.[4] This system was heavily conditioned by court decisions and authors' doctrines, and its sources were numerous: (i) local laws, either consuetudinary or statute-based, (ii) the laws of the sovereign (in the case of Malta, the *costituzioni*[5] and other laws compiled in the Municipal Code), and (iii) the Romano-canonical *ius commune* which served as a framework for the entire system.[6] The *ius commune* was transnational by definition: it was the doctrinal system – created by the European universities on the basis of Emperor Justinian's (482-565 CE) great

3 Published by Prince Grand Master Emanuel de Rohan (r 1775-1797) and thus referred to as the 'Code (of) Rohan', 'Code de Rohan', or 'Codice di Rohan'.

4 The term 'jurisprudence' in English has numerous meanings, such as the equivalent of 'philosophy of law' and 'legal theory'. At times, it is also used as the equivalent of the French '*jurisprudence*' and the Italian '*giurisprudenza*' (see RHS Tur (1978), 'What is Jurisprudence?' 1 28 *The Philosophical Quarterly* 111, 149), because the Anglo-Saxon 'case-law' has implications that *jurisprudence* and *giurisprudenza* do not have in their contemporary incarnation. In olden times, when continental Europe was still under the *Ancien Régime, jurisprudence* had a meaning similar to 'case-law' or, as Jeremy Bentham called it, 'judge-made law'. However, this is an interpretation that benefits from historical hindsight, in the sense that it defines the term *in comparison to* other terms; for contemporaries there were no other terms to compare to – the word referred to the system and, as is symptomatic of all systems, the system necessarily implied that there was no alternative to it – because the judges had more power than the weak, centralised State to make the law. The *Dictionnaire de l'Académie Française* of 1762 (Paris), for instance, defines '*jurisprudence*' as '*la science du Droit*', without making it explicit that the law was heavily conditioned by judges (as opposed to being made exclusively, or almost exclusively, by a different branch of the State). Compare this implicit assumption to the explicitation made in the present-day *Dictionnaire de l'Académie Française,* that to the first meaning ('*la science du droit et des lois*') adds a second: '*Ensemble des décisions de justice rendues dans une matière du droit ; solution d'une question de droit consacrée par les tribunaux ; usage, habitude que les juridictions établissent, par leurs décisions, d'interpréter et d'appliquer la loi de telle ou telle façon*'.

5 '*Costituzione*' meant 'rule' (equivalent of the Latin *regula*). See, for instance, the *Vocabolario Italiano e Latino* (1770) Padua.

6 Ettore Dezza (2001), '"Per li tempi d'avvenire siano abolite le torture". Note sulla disciplina del processo penale nel Codice Municipale di Malta del 1784' in Ettore Dezza (ed), *Saggi di Storia del Processo Penale nell'Età della Codificazione*, Padua: CEDAM, 6.

codification rediscovered at the turn of the millennium – that was common to all of Latin Christendom. Since the laws of Justinian were in Latin, Latin became the language (written and spoken) of all Western European scholars, and this re-discovered Roman law became the law common to all jurists capable of going beyond 'national' frontiers. From this neo-Roman law sprung the canon law.[7]

Analysing the Municipal Code, Ettore Dezza[8] expresses his admiration for the modern-looking technique used in its drafting: its provisions are clear and avoid philosophical or doctrinal digressions and justifications.[9] That said, the Code lacked rules that holistically defined the steps to be followed in criminal proceedings and assumed that the reader already knew the procedure;[10] the few procedural rules found in the Code were limited to individual parts of the proceedings.[11]

Being a compilation of laws and norms, it was not a 'code' in the modern sense of the word. The Municipal Code compiled civil, criminal, and other laws in one book; the modern Code deals exclusively with only one domain,[12] in our case, criminal law, implying a political organisation of society.[13] It does so not by merely collecting pre-existent legislative material but by containing new legislation,[14] by which one could understand old legislation being infused with a new spirit or the meaning of which being

---

7 Raoul van Caenegem (2002), *I sistemi giuridici europei* (Emmanuela Bertucci tr, il Mulino 2003) 21–22. The English-language version of this book is entitled, *European Law in the Past and the Future,* Cambridge: Cambridge University Press.

8 Professor of Legal History at the University of Pavia.

9 Dezza (2001) 6, 12–13.

10 § VI of the First Chapter of Book Two: '*La compilazione de' processi, e la procedura in materie criminali* [...] *dovrà essere quella medesima, che sin ora si è praticata, a riserva de' casi eccettuati in questa nuova compilazione*'. This is the late-*ius-commune* Romano-canonical inquisitorial procedure.

11 Dezza, 13. This followed the model then prevailing in Europe, as exemplified by the first 'modern' code, the Code of Tuscany, also known as the *Leopoldina.*

12 Mario E. Viora (1967), *Consolidazioni e Codificazioni: Contributo alla storia della codificazione,* Turin: Giappichelli (3rd edn.), 35; Giovanni Tarello (1976), *Storia della cultura giuridica moderna. Assolutismo e codificazione del diritto,* Bologna: il Mulino, 21.

13 Tarello, 21.

14 Viora, 41.

bent to accommodate new political realities.[15] The systematisation of the law, too, was innovative.[16] It has been claimed that modern codification was born as an alternative system opposed to the *ius commune*, the legal system of the *Ancien Régime*.[17]

The Codification movement

In the second half of the eighteenth century, a movement came into being in Europe that called for a reform inspired by the Enlightenment *philosophes* and based on the codification of the criminal law. It was a reaction against the system then obtaining in Europe, one of the main features of which had been the existence of a 'common law' (*ius commune*) of crimes. The new movement aimed to codify the principles of natural law, 'valid for all the peoples on earth according to Montesquieu',[18] while each codification effort was 'national in spirit'.[19] This spirit disappeared by the nineteenth century, by which time codifications attempted solely to 'express purely national truths or to serve purely national needs'.[20]

The movement for the codification of the criminal law can be divided into three historical periods, of which only the first two interest us here: the first dating roughly from 1748 (when Montesquieu's *De l'esprit des lois* was published) to 1813 (the year the Bavarian Code was promulgated) and the second, from 1815 to 1867 when the Belgian Code was promulgated.[21] The former was characterised by Montesquieu's (1689-1755) preoccupation with the reconciliation of positive and natural law; the latter by Jeremy Bentham's (1748-1832) concern with the utilitarian character of the provisions of substantive law.[22] The movement then took a strictly liberal turn, 'aiming at the lessening of sentences and the abolition

15 *Ibid.*

16 Tarello, 21.

17 Pio Caroni (1998), *Saggi sulla storia della codificazione*, Milan: Giuffrè, 39.

18 Charles-Louis de Secondat, Baron de La Brède et de Montesquieu.

19 LB Schwartz (1958), 'The Collection of European Penal Codes and the Study of Comparative Law' (1958) 106 (3) *University of Pennsylvania Law Review* 341.

20 *Ibid.*

21 *Ibid.*, 346. The third and last period spans from the Belgian Penal Code of 1867 to the promulgation of the Italian Code of 1889. *Ibid* 349.

22 Schwartz, 346.

of certain punishments incompatible with the idea, henceforth held, of the dignity of man'.[23]

The legal system had come under heavy fire during the eighteenth century, when the Enlightenment movement began its campaign for the systematisation of the criminal law and for legal certainty, arguing that the evolution of criminal law should be tied to the political evolution of society. The most famous Enlightenment thinker in this context, Cesare Beccaria (1738-1794), demolished the criminal system of his times with his famous essay *On Crimes and Punishments* of 1764.[24]

But did the principles of the Enlightenment and rationalism – advocated by Beccaria and his followers – trigger a complete scientific rupture with the past and with tradition? According to Aniceto Masferrer,[25] 'this account is more a fairy tale than a credible account of the historical truth (to the extent history has – or should have – any relation to truth or objectivity)'.[26] This view is shared by Alberto Cadoppi,[27] who argues that modern criminal law did not begin with Beccaria, but throughout the nineteenth century (probably until the enactment of the Zanardelli Code in 1889), the approach to criminal law was a precipitate of the doctrines inspired by the *ius commune* and their dogmatic re-hashing by the more influential criminal lawyers of the latter half of the eighteenth century.[28] He has argued that the ideas of the

23 *Ibid.*, 349.

24 The opening lines set the tone for the debate: 'Some remains of the laws of an ancient people, compiled on the authority of a prince who reigned twelve centuries ago in Constantinople, later mingled with Lombard customs and collected in hodge-podge volumes by unofficial and obscure commentators – this is what forms the traditional opinions that in a large part of Europe are nonetheless called 'law'. Moreover, it is today as pernicious as it is common that an opinion of Carpzov, or an ancient custom cited by Claro, or a torture suggested with irate complacency by Farinacci should be the laws unhesitatingly followed by those who ought to dispose of the lives and fortunes of men only with diffidence'. Cesare Beccaria, *On Crimes and Punishments* (David Young tr, Hackett Publishing 1986 [1764]) 1.

25 Professor of Legal History at the University of Valencia.

26 Aniceto Masferrer, 'Tradition and Foreign Influences in the 19th Century Codification of Criminal Law: Dispelling the Myth of the Pervasive French Influence in Europe and Latin America' in Aniceto Masferrer (ed) (2018), *The Western Codification of Criminal Law*, Berlin: Springer International Publishing, 5.

27 Professor of Legal History at the University of Parma.

28 Alberto Cadoppi (2001), *Materiali per un'introduzione allo studio del Diritto Penale Comparato*, Padua: CEDAM, 155.

Enlightenment referenced by Beccaria's famous 'manifesto' of criminal law but articulated in terms of legal doctrine by Gaetano Filangieri (1752-1788) and Mario Pagano (1748-1799) did not replace the doctrinal achievements that the *ius commune* scholars had matured over the centuries.[29] Cadoppi ropes in another important Italian jurist, Adriano Cavanna (1938-2002), who had argued that the thinkers of the Enlightenment, while insisting on a renewal of the criminal law and on moving on from its traditional defects, still placed their trust in the doctrinal legacy of the great legal interpreters of the sixteenth and seventeenth centuries.[30]

One oft-overlooked aspect of the history of criminal law is that the major issue concerning criminal law at the beginning of the nineteenth century – and thus at the moment that modern codification was gaining momentum – was not scientific but political. Indeed, as RC van Caenegem (1927-2018) pointed out, 'no study of criminal law, in the past or in the present, can be conducted fruitfully without constant reference to the political situation and the power structure in society: criminal law is not the fruit of logical deductions from eternal principles formulated by unworldly scholars'.[31] This, argues Masferrer, explains the harshness of the legislation, the severity of the punishments (sometimes even affecting those who had not committed the crime), the rare or inconsistent application of punishments (confiscation of goods, infamy, the death penalty), the disproportion between crime and punishment, the persistence of torture in spite of its rare application – all these depended on political expediency, not on legislative necessity.[32] *Ancien Régime* lawyers had actually known and defended principles that we now consider as 'modern', such as the principle of legality, proportionality, favourable interpretation, the presumption of innocence, and that were the cornerstone of the arguments made by Beccaria, Montesquieu, and the other thinkers of the Enlightenment – what had happened was that these principles had not been politically recognised or implemented.[33]

Masferrer argues that this *political* shift had indeed been a severance

29 *Ibid.*, 155.

30 *Ibid.*, 156.

31 Raoul van Caenegem (1991), 'Criminal Law in England and Flanders under King Henry II and Count Philip of Alsace' in RC van Caenegem (ed), *Legal History: A European Perspective*, London: The Hambledon Press, 60.

32 Masferrer (2018), 6.

33 *Ibid.*, 7.

from tradition.[34] The great contribution of the codification movement to criminal law can be summed up in three terms: systematisation, humanisation, and secularisation[35] – these are facets of a political re-orientation rather than a ‘scientific revolution’.

The climate in some parts of the Italian-speaking legal ecosystem

In this section, I shall zero in on those jurisdictions in the Italian-speaking area of Europe which presumably influenced Maltese jurists. I am not aware of any study that has tried to explore the cultural ties between the Maltese legal profession and the Italian peninsula in the period under review, ie, the 70-odd years prior to the promulgation of the Criminal Code in 1854.[36] It has been claimed[37] that in the 1830s, Maltese students attended the University of Pisa, but I have not been able to ascertain the validity of this claim. From the *Dictionary of Maltese Biographies*, it transpires that two jurists did indeed study at the University of Pisa: Lorenzo de Caro (1817-1853) studied under Giovanni Carmignani (1768-1847) and graduated in jurisprudence, and was later appointed professor of Philosophy; Giuseppe Randon (1807-1892), after completing his JUD at the University of Malta in 1831, furthered his studies in Pisa, and upon returning to Malta in 1833, was appointed to the Chair of Criminal Law, which he occupied until 1839. There is also Ferdinando Caruana Dingli (1798-1870), Professor of International and Constitutional Law at the University of Malta, who translated Giovanni Carmignani’s *Elementi di Diritto Criminali* from Latin.[38] Yet, two students and a translation do not one whole generation make.

---

34 *Ibid.*, 9.

35 *Ibid.*, 17.

36 I am probably echoing former European Court of Human Rights Judge Giovanni Bonello who, at least twice, pointed out that there is no proper history of the legal professions in Malta. See Giovanni Bonello (2000), ‘For a History of Lawyering in Malta’ in Giovanni Bonello, *Histories of Malta: Deceptions and Perceptions*, Fondazzjoni Patrimonju Malti, Vol 1, 260-62, and Giovanni Bonello (2007), ‘Notes for a History of the Judiciary at the time of the Order’ https://judiciary.mt/en/Documents/PDF/A%20History%20of%20the%20Judiciary.pdf, accessed 15 October 2021. There are Paul Saliba’s (1996) *A Manual for Legal Procurators*, Malta: PEG, and Michael Refalo’s (2014), *The Maltese Nineteenth-Century Notary And His Archives*, Malta: BDL, but more still needs to be done.

37 Cadoppi, 368.

38 Published in Malta for the first time in 1847 and then re-issued numerous times in Italy.

The closest affinity was with the nearest Italian State: Naples/Two Sicilies, as indirectly confirmed by Hugh Harding[39] when he quotes the 1832 Maltese Commission entrusted with the Project of the Penal Code, putting forward the argument that,

> Malta was then[40] governed by the legislation [...] prevailing in that neighbouring Italian state before the promulgation of its Code, that Malta had shared for centuries with it a common fate and the same sovereignty, that the language of the Maltese tribunals and of the Maltese law was the language of the tribunals and laws of Naples.[41]

This cursory look at the Italian-speaking world will therefore be limited to Naples and Sicily and, out of historical necessity, to the Ionian Islands. But first, reference should be made to the first code that reflected the principles of the codification movement, namely the so-called *Leopoldina*, promulgated in Pisa in 1786 by Leopold II of Tuscany.[42] It had been drawn up by a commission headed by Beccaria himself, was based on the general principle of legality (offences to be established in advance), and abolished torture, general confiscation, capital punishment, and branding.[43]

---

39 (1925-2014), lecturer in History of Legislation at the University of Malta from 1950 onwards.

40 ie, prior to the British occupation.

41 Hugh W Harding (1980 [1968]), *Maltese Legal History under British Rule (1801-1836)*, Malta: Malta University Press, 359-60.

42 The *Codice Leopoldo* was the reform of Tuscan Criminal Law carried out by Leopold, Grand Duke of Tuscany in 1786. A survey of the topic includes Adam Wandruszka, *Pietro Leopoldo, un grande riformatore* (Vallecchi 1968); Mario Mattolini, *Il principe illuminato Pietro Leopoldo: la Toscana dei Lorena* (Medicea 1981); Floriana Colao, *La giustizia criminale senese nell'età delle riforme leopoldine: post tenebras spero lucem* (Giuffrè 1989); Dario Zuliani, *La riforma penale di Pietro Leopoldo. Presentazione storica e indice delle edizioni della Legge toscana del 30 novembre 1786* (Giuffrè 1995); Giorgio La Rosa, *Il sigillo delle riforme: la Costituzione di Pietro Leopoldo di Toscana* (Vita e pensiero 1997); Monica Chiantini, 'Diritto e processo penale alla fine dell'*Ancien Régime*' in Mario Ascheri (ed), *Lezioni di storia della codificazione e delle costituzioni* (Giappichelli 2008) 41–43; Daniele Edigati, *Prima della "Leopoldina": la giustizia criminale toscana tra prassi e riforme legislative nel XVIII secolo* (Jovene 2011); Vittorio Parlato, 'Pietro Leopoldo: Un Principe Riformatore' (2016) 67 (3–4) *Studi urbinati, scienze giuridiche, politiche ed economiche* 399-416; P Francesco Listri, *Pietro Leopoldo: Granduca di Toscana, un riformatore del Settecento* (Leonardo 2016).

43 Schwartz, 344.

In the late eighteenth century, Naples was run by the reformist Bernardo Tanucci (1698-1783), who tried to re-organise the traditional normative materials but could not overcome the conservative spirit of the Commission entrusted with the work. He did, however, manage to reform the judiciary, imposing the obligation of motivating judgments.[44] The judges of the superior courts were ordered to limit themselves to the express laws of the Kingdom and the 'common laws' (the *ius commune*) in their motivations and to avoid the *'nude autorità de' dottori'* and their own decisions (*'giurisprudenza'*).[45] In case of *lacunae,* the *giusdicenti* (literally, those who say what the law is) should revert to the sovereign, following the model of the French Revolution's *référé législatif.* The Courts, however, resisted this innovation with all their might, and it had to be revoked before a few years had passed.[46] There were moments when Naples followed Enlightenment principles: torture, for instance, though not abolished, was not resorted to either after 1738. However, Naples remained incapable of reform, piling up the pressure that then detonated as the Parthenopean Republic of 1799.[47]

Beccaria's fame spread like wildfire across Europe, mostly because his book was a huge publishing success. Yet, he was not the only one to advocate the humanisation of criminal law (in particular, the abolition of torture and capital punishment). In Naples, say, even a minor exponent of the Neapolitan Enlightenment like Tommaso Briganti (1691-1762) was decidedly against the use of torture.[48] Naples, however, produced the more renowned Gaetano Filangieri and Mario Pagano, whose *Scienza della legislazione* (1784) and *Considerazioni sopra il processo criminale* (1787) respectively remain bulwarks of Enlightened thought.[49]

---

44 Chiantini, 40.

45 *Ibid.* [bare authority of doctors of law]. The quotation continues, '*che hanno purtroppo, colle loro opinioni, o alterato o reso incerto ed arbitrario il diritto*'.

46 *Ibid.*

47 *Ibid.*, 41. The jurist Pagano was one of the members of the Government of this very short-lived Republic. On the Parthenopean Republic, see Silvio Maurano (1971), *La repubblica partenopea,* Milan: Ceschina.

48 See Tommaso Briganti (1842 [1755]), *Pratica Criminale,* Naples: Gabriele Marotta Libraio Editore, Vol 2, 32–33.

49 For an overview of the intellectual climate in Naples leading up to this time, see John Robertson (2005), *The Case for The Enlightenment: Scotland and Naples 1680-1760,* Cambridge: Cambridge University Press.

The Kingdom of Naples was divided into two parts:[50] the Neapolitan (or continental) part[51] and Sicily.[52] Despite widespread censorship, the winds of Enlightenment thinking swept over eighteenth-century Sicily too. The Palermitan Tommaso Natale (1733-1819)[53] published in Palermo in 1772 his *Riflessioni politiche intorno all'efficacia e necessità delle pene*, a book that earned him both fame and a place among the more important thinkers of the Enlightenment advocating for a renewal of the criminal law. His thinking is similar to Beccaria's: both insisted on more humane punishments inspired by their utilitarian vision of criminal law, on the proportionality of the punishment, against torture as a method of acquiring evidence, and against the death penalty (even though he believed it should still be used, for instance, in crimes against the government). He believed that it is in the interests of the community to have an effective educational system that should be both public and secular, as this would avoid crimes. This idea puts Natale among the major *Illuministi* of Italy, like the Neapolitan Antonio Genovesi (1713-1769), and the major European ones, like Montesquieu. Natale took great pride in underlining the fact that he wrote his book in 1758, that is to say, five years before Beccaria wrote his.

The Neapolitan Penal Code of 1808[54] was a milestone in the attempt

---

50 It also had feudal ties with Ragusa (modern-day Dubrovnik).

51 '*Al di qua del Faro*': this side of the Lighthouse (of Messina) – the stretch of sea between mainland Italy and Sicily now referred to as the Strait of Messina. This part of the Kingdom occupied mainland Italy and comprised lands from the Abruzzi down to the Calabrie, as well as the enclave of the *Stato dei Presidi* (next to Tuscany). Giuseppe Orlandi (1996), 'Il Regno di Napoli nel Settecento' (1996) 44 (1) *Spicilegium Historicum Congregationis SSmi Redemptoris* 11–12.

52 '*Di là del Faro*': beyond the Lighthouse (of Messina), ie Sicily and its islands. Ibid.

53 Natale was the son of a Marquis descended from a rich merchant family from Cosenza (in Calabria) and a Messinese noblewoman. He was a member of the Council of State, a member of the *Tribunale del Real Patrimonio*, deputy of the Kingdom of Sicily, member of the Council of the Supreme Magistracy for commerce, and deputy at the University of Palermo, even though he never taught there.

54 It has been described as endowed with a high level of technical perfection, and that whereas history imposes that it be referred to as the laws of Joseph Bonaparte for the Kingdom of Naples, it would be closer to the truth to say that they were the laws drawn up by the Neapolitans for the Kingdom of Joseph Bonaparte. Sergio Vinciguerra (1996), 'Una penalistica italiana al servizio della politica francese: le leggi penali di Giuseppe Bonaparte per il Regno di Napoli (1808)' in Sergio Vinciguerra (ed), *Le Leggi Penali di Giuseppe Bonaparte per il Regno di Napoli*

to systematise the powerful albeit fragmentary knowledge amassed by legal science on the foundations of 'Roman' law. It disregarded the role Montesquieu intended for the judge[55] and instead embraced the *Ancien Régime* idea that the law spoke through the judge's mouth.[56] It retained certain aspects of the punishment system of the past and in other instances – despite the fact that this was the *French* Kingdom of Naples – it preferred local solutions inspired by the *ius commune* to French novel solutions.[57] There is a slight element of continuity between this Code of 1808 and the 1819 Code for the Kingdom of the Two Sicilies.[58]

Following the end of the English quinquennium in Sicily[59] and the end of the Napoleonic Wars, the Bourbon King returned to the throne of the Two Sicilies in 1816. Naples had already had a new Code in 1808; Sicily was still ruled by an older set of criminal laws.[60] The King ordered that a newer Code be drafted for the entire Kingdom and tasked a commission made up of jurists who had all been Joachim Murat's collaborators during Murat's reign (1767-1815)[61] as King of Naples (1808-1815).[62] The Commission drew inspiration from the French Penal Code of 1810 and, to a lesser extent, from the Austrian Criminal Code of 1803 and the Draft Criminal Code for the

(1808), Padua: CEDAM, X.

55 *'Que la bouche qui pronounce les paroles de la loi, des êtres inanimés qui n'en peuvent modérer ni la force ni la rigueur'*. Montesquieu (2008), *De l'esprit des lois* (V Goldschmidt ed), Paris: Flammarion, 252.

56 Vinciguerra, xviii.

57 Mario Da Passano (1996), 'La codificazione del diritto penale a Napoli nel periodo francese' in Sergio Vinciguerra (ed), *Le Leggi Penali di Giuseppe Bonaparte per il Regno di Napoli (1808)*, Padua: CEDAM, clxiv.

58 *Ibid.*, clxx.

59 On the British constitutional experiments in Sicily between 1810 and 1815, see John Rosselli, *Lord William Bentinck and the British Occupation of Sicily 1811-1814* (CUP 1956); John Rosselli, *Lord William Bentinck: The making of a Liberal Imperialist* (Sussex University Press 1974); and Mark A Sammut, 'Historical Facts and Myths surrounding the Criminal Code of Malta' in Mark A Sammut, *Essays in Maltese Legal History and Comparative Law* (Oxford Legal Publishing 2017) vol 1, 20–22.

60 Article 3, Decree for the Promulgation of the Criminal Code, 21 May 1819.

61 Joachim Murat was Napoleon's brother-in-law.

62 Raffaele Feola (1977), *Dall'Illuminismo alla Restaurazione: Donato Tommasi e la legislazione delle Sicilie*, Naples: Jovene, 197.

(Napoleonic) Kingdom of Italy of 1806. However, all in all, the Code was a result of the evolution that had begun with the Law on offences and penalties of 1808 that incorporated ideas by Filangieri, Pagano, and Gian Domenico Romagnosi (1761-1835), the amendments made by Murat in 1812, and the influence of Italian criminal jurists.[63] Though not an absolute innovation, the Code of 1819 had a national character, and in certain aspects, it was original – unquestionably, it was an improvement on the 1810 French Code.[64]

That said, the 1819 Code was the expression of an absolutist, monarchical, and confessional State. It reflected the alliance between Throne and Altar, the former offering the highest level of protection to the latter in return for the highest level of political loyalty.[65] At the same time, it was more progressive with respect to the French model, in particular with regard to the humanisation of punishments.[66]

At one point in time, the drafters of the Maltese Code identified the Code of the Ionian Islands for possible adaptation and promulgation as the Criminal Code for Malta.[67] This Code, also written in Italian[68] (and therefore accessible to the Maltese), on the one hand did away with judicial arbitrariness – an *Ancien Régime* characteristic – by introducing the principles of legality and certainty of law; on the other hand, it kept the death penalty and,

---

63 Ugo Spirito (1974), *Storia del diritto penale italiano: da Cesare Beccaria ai nostri giorni*, Milan: Sansoni, 65.

64 Sergio Vinciguerra (1999), *Diritto penale italiano: Concetto, fonti, validità, interpretazione*, Vol 1, Padua: CEDAM, 245.

65 Sergio Vinciguerra (1994), 'Una tecnica giuridica raffinata per l'assolutismo regio' in Sergio Vinguerra and Mario Da Passano (eds), *Codice per lo Regno delle Due Sicilie (1819), Parte Seconda: Le Leggi Penali*, Padua: CEDAM, xii–xiii.

66 *Ibid.*, xviii.

67 Harding, 348; Andrew Jameson (1844), *Report on the Proposed Code of Criminal Laws for the Island of Malta and its Dependencies*, Malta: Malta Government Printing Press, 3.

68 Even though art 4, ch 1 of the 1817 Constitution of the United States of the Ionian Islands laid down that the 'language of these States is Greek'. Quoted by Sergio Vinciguerra (2008), 'Umanità delle pene detentive, prevenzione del reato e ristoro del danno' in Sergio Vinciguerra (ed), *Codice Penale degli Stati Uniti delle Isole Jonie (1841)*, Padua: CEDAM, xii. For more information on the Ionian Islands during this period, see Sakis Gekas (2017), *Xenocracy: State, Class and Colonialism in the Ionian Islands, 1815-1864*, Oxford: Berghahn, and Konstantina Zanou (2018), *Transnational Patriotism in the Mediterranean, 1800-1850*, Oxford: Oxford University Press.

generally speaking, reflected an authoritarian approach. Its only elements to reflect Enlightenment thinking were the guarantees afforded the accused and legality; humanisation is completely disregarded.[69] There are clear influences of Romagnosi's code of penal procedure that came into effect in the Napoleonic Kingdom of Italy in 1807, though these influences are perhaps refracted by the 1819 Code of the Two Sicilies.[70] While the Code did receive four rules from English procedure (ie, hearsay rule, opinion rule, privilege against self-incrimination, and guilty plea),[71] these rules seem almost lost in the open sea of a procedure that looks nothing but Continental.[72] And yet, their presence alters the entire make-up of the Code, investing it with more guarantees for the accused.[73]

Riccardo Ferrante[74] has made an observation highlighting a problem that is also relevant to Malta. He stated that while there was in the Ionian Islands a desire definitively to break away from the Venetian jurisprudential tradition that, owing to historical reasons, had been imposed on them, it does seem incongruous that they requested codification from the English![75]

England

England was the 'traditional citadel of unwritten law, or at least uncodified law', but in the first half of the nineteenth century, 'for the first

---

69 Mario Alessandro Cattaneo (2008), 'Un codice penale post-illuminista' in Sergio Vinciguerra (ed), *Codice Penale degli Stati Uniti delle Isole Jonie (1841)*, Padua: CEDAM, lxxxiv.

70 Ettore Dezza (2008), '"La corte vi domanda se siete reo o innocente". Istituti di *Common Law* nel codice di procedura penale degli Stati Uniti delle Isole Jonie (1844)' in Sergio Vinciguerra (ed), *Codice Penale degli Stati Uniti delle Isole Jonie (1841)*, Padua: CEDAM, clxxi–clxxii.

71 *Ibid.*, clxxiii.

72 *Ibid.*, clxxxii.

73 *Ibid.*, clxxxii. These rules seem like a snapshot of 1830s English procedural law, implying that their presence is due to neither second-hand nor ideological origins, but to personal courtroom experience, possibly of the British lawyers involved in the Code's drafting. *Ibid.*, clxxxiv.

74 Professor of Legal History at the University of Genoa.

75 Riccardo Ferrante (2008), '"Padroni dell'uso de' capitali senza le leggi proibitive degli altri governi". Diritto penale ed economia nelle Isole Ionie' in Sergio Vinciguerra (ed), *Codice Penale degli Stati Uniti delle Isole Jonie (1841)*, Padua: CEDAM, cli.

[...] time in its history, [it was] sensitive to the movement for codification'.[76] In 1833, the Royal Commission on the Criminal Law[77] was directed by Parliament to explore the possibility of codifying all of the criminal law; in other words, to ascertain whether it was feasible to put together in one enactment both the statute law and common law elements. In its First Report (1834), the Commission expressed strong support for the codification goal, but by the time of the Seventh Report (1843), it was arguing that the common law achieved more coherence and sophistication than the statute law in treating crime. Nothing came out of all this – in 1854, the common law judges expressed their opposition, and the project was dropped owing to what one of the members of the Commission called 'Codiphobia'.[78] The English were keen on seeing codification charity begin elsewhere, not at home.

The intellectual climate in Malta

The drafters of the Maltese Codes always had all of this at the back of their minds. This was the legal world of their times, the backdrop which offered them conscious or unconscious points of reference.

The 'code'[79] that the Knights had bequeathed them 'retained the defects making up the legacy of the *ius commune*: the multiplicity of and confusion in the sources of procedural law, the complex and formalistic structure of the judicial apparatus, the chaos reigning in jurisdictions'.[80] Its main author

---

76 Schwartz, 353.

77 This Commission included John Austin (1790-1859), Jeremy Bentham's disciple, and 'Father of Legal Positivism'. Austin had two connections with Malta. He served under Lord William Bentinck (1774-1839) in Sicily and in Malta (Wilfrid E Rumble (2005), *Doing Austin Justice: The Reception of John Austin's Philosophy of Law in Nineteenth-Century England*, London: Continuum, 13) and he participated in the Royal Commission to Malta, to which he was appointed in 1836. The reports he co-wrote in this context are probably 'his greatest accomplishment'. *Ibid.*, 21. A recent analysis of Austin's *Reports* can be found in Daniela Formosa (2017), 'The 1836 Austin and Lewis Commission: An Analytical Review of Private Correspondences and Reports' (unpublished BA thesis, University of Malta).

78 David Lieberman (2009), *The Challenge of Codification in English Legal History*, Tokyo: Research Institute of Economy, Trade and Industry, 11-12. For a differently nuanced analysis, see also Aniceto Masferrer (2019), 'French Codification and 'Codiphobia' in Common Law Traditions', 34 *The Tulane European and Civil Law Forum* 1–31.

79 Dezza, 5, '*collezione normativa*' [a normative collection].

80 The original in Italian reads: 'conserva quei difetti propri dell'eredità del

– the Neapolitan Giandonato Rogadeo (1718-1784) – did not hold Beccaria in high esteem;[81] but neither did his main Maltese detractors. In his *Apologia* (a counterattack on Rogadeo's criticism of the Maltese legal professions), the *uditore* Gian Nicolò Muscat (1735-1803) writes that Rogadeo did not need to waste time writing in favour of torture and the death penalty as he was preaching to the converted.[82] Another detractor, Baron Pisani,[83] however, defends Beccaria[84] in his *Lettera di un maltese* and even expresses strong objections to torture,[85] and yet, all said and done, he still thinks that torture should be resorted to in certain cases[86] and that capital punishment should be imposed, though not frequently.[87] And yet, the Municipal Code lays down that 'for the future, all tortures and torment shall be abolished'.[88] This abolition,

---

diritto comune che [...] possiamo riassumere nella molteplicità e confusione delle fonti del processo, nella struttura complessa e formalistica dell'apparato giudiziario, nel caos delle giurisdizioni'. Claudio Carcereri de Prati (2001), 'Introduzione: Le riforme giudiziarie a Malta nella second metà del XVIII secolo' in Nicola Picardi and Alessandro Giuliani (eds), *Codice di Malta 1777/1784*, Milan: Giuffrè, xxix.

81 See Gian Donato Rogadeo (1783), *Ragionamenti del Cavaliere Giandonato Rogadeo sul Regolamento della Giustizia, e sulle Pene*, Naples, for instance 216–21 and 324–30, for his attack on Beccaria (and Voltaire) on the issues of torture and capital punishment, respectively.

82 Gio Nicolò Muscat (1783), *Apologia a favore dell'Inclita Nazione Maltese*, Rome, v. On Muscat, see Giovanni Bonello (2016), 'A Mild Debunking of Dr Gio Nicolò Muscat' (2016) XVII *Melita Historica* 17–18, and for opposing views, Frans Ciappara (2018), *Church-State Relations in Late-Eighteenth-Century Malta*, Malta: Malta University Press.

83 I was unable to find the dates of birth and death of the Baron.

84 Gaetano Pisani (1783), *Lettera di un maltese ad un Cavaliere Gerosolomitano Professo su i Cinque Ragionamenti del Cavalier Giandonato Rogadeo*, Vercelli, 128-29. Pisani also quotes Natale ('il Marchese di Monte Rosato') (*ibid.*, 97), and mentions Antonio Genovesi, the Neapolitan Illuminist priest considered one of the main exponents of the Southern Italian Enlightenment, who wrote about economics and other subjects not related to law (*ibid.*, 124). About Genovesi, see Mario Agrimi (1967), 'Antonio Genovesi e l'Illuminismo riformatore nel Mezzogiorno' 22 (4) *Belfagor* 373–410.

85 Pisani, 128-32. Incidentally, the Baron provides the curriculum that the eighteenth-century (Maltese) law student followed: Justinian, the Pandects, Bynkershoek, and Samuel Coccejo (*ibid.*, 133).

86 *Ibid.*, 134.

87 *Ibid.*, 135–44.

88 The original in Italian reads: '*per li tempi d'avvenire siano abolite le torture, e qualsisiano tormenti*'. § XXVI of the First Chapter of Book Two. This provi-

however, was not meant to cover cases of *lese majesté,* parricides, murders, and other crimes that impacted public tranquillity and safety.[89]

Like their compatriots of the late eighteenth century, the Maltese jurists of the early nineteenth century were fully aware of their *Zeitgeist.* Referring to the 1836 Draft of the Maltese Criminal Code, Mario Da Passano (1946-2005)[90] observed that the work was the result also of deep knowledge of the developments in penal codification and the discussions on doctrine that were taking place in continental Europe at the time, in addition to a deep knowledge of Maltese law.[91] It is thus clearly reasonable to presume that the Maltese were fully aware that France was the first continental country to experience a liberal revolution and that Napoleon's criminal code was the first liberal code of Europe; 'liberal' referred to national sovereignty (as opposed to absolute monarchy) – that is to say, the separation of the person of the Sovereign and the State – and to the principles of legality and equality. The French Code was translated into many languages, even though the translations are not the primary linguistic reason for its widespread reception as, at the time, French was the most widely known language in Europe.[92] Because of this, all countries had to consult the French Code before codifying, and on account of its great influence, common law lawyers 'erroneously regarded [the French Code] as the "continental model" of codification'.[93]

Continuation of the *ius commune*?

Given this participation in the intellectual *Zeitgeist,* it might seem bizarre that the Commission[94] that drew up the Draft of 1836[95] should argue

---

sion appears in both the 1784 and the 1843 editions of the Code.

89 § XXVII.

90 Professor Legal History at the University of Sassari.

91 Mario Da Passano (2003), 'Le *Leggi Penali* Napoletane e il Primo Progetto di Codice Penale Maltese (1836)' in Sergio Vinciguerra (ed), *Leggi Criminali per l'Isola di Malta e Sue Dipendenza (1854),* Padua: CEDAM, lxxvi.

92 Masferrer, 23.

93 *Ibid.*

94 Composed of CV Bonnici, IG Bonavita, GF Falson, F Torriggiani, and F Chapelle.

95 For a number of reasons, this Draft was never enacted. See Albert Ganado (2003), *La storia del codice penale di Malta del 1854. Un breve ragguaglio* in Sergio Vinciguerra (ed), *Leggi Criminali per l'Isola di Malta e Sue Dipendenze (1854),* Padua: CEDAM, xxix–xlii.

that the French archetype, and thus its Neapolitan derivate, were based 'on Roman laws and court decisions, recognised in all of France, and obtaining in the greater part of it, and in the Two Sicilies, even before the codes promulgated in the latter, and in the former'.[96] The Commission further argued that, accordingly, the Maltese Draft, being modelled on the French and Neapolitan Codes, conserved the principles of the Roman jurists, and, since the Roman law was one of the sources of Maltese law, 'the Draft is less of a change in the essence, so to speak, of the present legislation of these islands, than a reduction of the same to a method, a more ordered system, and this to ensure that its administration has a more certain effect'.[97]

Da Passano observes that the historical rendition given by the Commission was a '*forzatura*': it imposed an arbitrary and debatable interpretation on the history of Maltese criminal law[98] – assuming, one should add, that we accept the narrative that codification meant a rupture with the former system.

It seems more likely, however, that the Commission's rendition agrees with the interpretation represented in this article by Masferrer and Cadoppi that the 'modern' criminal law was a continuation of the *ius commune* system adjusted to new philosophical inclinations. Indeed, van Caenegem points out that in reality, despite the fact that the Roman law had been abolished together with all the other sources of law of the *Ancien Régime*, the judges of nineteenth-century Europe did not hesitate to refer to it in their judgments and to demonstrate a deep knowledge of Justinian's law that, incidentally, the universities had never stopped teaching.[99] This would certainly call for further investigation with regard to the Maltese context.

---

96 The original in Italian reads: 'sulle leggi, e sulla giurisprudenza Romana, riconosciute in tutta la Francia, e prevalenti in gran parte della medesima, e nelle Due Sicilie, prima dei codici promulgati in queste, ed in quella'. *Rapporto dei Commissarj di Sua Maestà per la formazione di Nuovi Codici di Legge, per l'Isola di Malta e sue Dipendenze, sui due Progetti, l'uno di Leggi Penali, e l'altro di Leggi di Organizzazione e Procedura Penale* (1835), Malta, xxviii.

97 The original in Italian reads: 'tale progetto perciò costituisce meno un cangiamento dell'essenza, se così si può dire, della attuale legislazione di queste isole, che una riduzione della stessa ad un metodo, e sistema meglio ordinato, e tale da assicurare alla sua amministrazione un effetto più certo'. *Ibid.*

98 Da Passano, lxxvii. See also Sammut, 34–45.

99 van Caenegem, 18.

What do we mean by 'Roman law' in the Maltese context? We find the answer in an anonymous book written by *'un Giovane Avvocato Maltese'*[100]: 'All penal provisions, customarily embraced by the courts of criminal jurisdiction, whether their origins lie in written Justinian Roman law or elsewhere'.[101] He points out that 'we often colloquially refer to the *ius commune* and customary law as Roman law, even though the Municipal Code carefully makes no reference to Roman and Justinian Law, but to the law [*ius*] called common [*commune*]'.[102]

The Maltese were engaged in constant funambulism. They were putting forward the argument that there was (once again) a common legal system in Europe despite the national character of the codifications, while being aware of the criticism made by the English judge John Richardson (1771-1841) in his 1826 Report on the Laws of Malta. They were, like Harlequin, trying to serve two masters at the same time: their own legal formation and the expectations of the foreign power 'protecting' their occupied homeland. In his Report, Richardson recommended that one of the reforms to Malta's criminal laws should be the abolition of all references to foreign authorities as a basis for judgment. Referring to 'points neither few nor inconsiderable not provided for by the [Municipal Code], constitutions, and Enactments,' Richardson pointed out that 'the general provisions of the Roman Law, and the decisions and precedents of Italian, Spanish, and other Foreign Tribunals, where that law has been established, and the comments of jurists thereon are admitted as authority'.[103] In his view,

> foreign decisions and commentaries [were] a mass of

---

100 Pseudonym meaning, 'A young Maltese lawyer'.

101 The original in Italian reads: *'qualsiasi disposizione penale, abbracciata per consuetudine ne' tribunali di giurisdizione criminale, sia che abbia avuto origine dal diritto scritto romano giustinianeo, sia da altre sorgenti'. Annotazioni alle Leggi Criminali per l'Isola di Malta e Sue Dipendenza da Servire di Guida al Giurato per cura d'un giovane Avvocato maltese* (1870), Malta: Tipo-Litografia Anglo-Maltese, 30.

102 The original in Italian reads: *'il diritto comune e consuetudinario (sovente presso di noi designato volgarmente col nome di* Diritto romano*), sebbene nel Diritto Municipale, non si fece più accuratamente mai riferenza al diritto romano e giustinianeo, ma al diritto detto comune'. Ibid.*

103 *Report respecting the Courts and the Administration of the Law at Malta; made by Sir John Richardson Knight His Majesty's Commissioner, 19 August 1826,* National Archives of Malta GMR 4, 70–71.

learning so vast and multifarious, that there are few points upon which authorities may not be found to support of both sides of the question.

It seemed [...] therefore to be desirable to recast and to renact [*sic*] the whole body of the Criminal Law in force in those Islands, and if possible to abolish all reference to foreign authorities, otherwise than by way of illustration or argument.[104]

The 1836 Draft laid down that all pre-existing laws would cease to have effect in those areas regulated by the new Code,[105] thereby apparently severing the umbilical cord with the former system. Moreover, the 1836 Commission recommended that the Draft Code it had drawn up, though inspired by (and mostly copied from) the Code of the Two Sicilies, should not be interpreted through the mediation of authors who commented on the latter Code, insisting on adopting a cautious approach. The reason for this, argued the Commission, was that 'since one of the principal characteristics of the modern code is the perfect concatenation of all its parts, if even a small rule found in the Sicilian Code was left out of the Maltese, or if something were introduced in the latter that is not found in the former, then the certainty that such opinions can be useful to understanding the Maltese code would

104 *Ibid.*, 72-73. Given the colonial context, 'foreign' needs to be properly construed.

105 *Disposizione preliminare*. Elsewhere the Draft Code left certain areas out of its purview, such as the lazaretto and quarantine, goldsmiths and silversmiths, and medical doctors and surgeons. A short while before the Code of Police Laws was promulgated in 1854, Mittermaier observed that the Maltese Police Laws were stricter than those applicable in England, especially in London in the sense that many acts are forbidden in Malta that are not punished in London, he observed. Furthermore, the penal provisions in Malta are more undefined and vague than those obtaining in England. He mentioned as examples doctors who do not render their services when requested (art 137) and doctors who use abbreviations or leave blank spaces in the prescriptions they write (art 139). Mittermaier (1853), 'Il Codice Maltese sulle contravvenzioni, e le leggi e regolamenti di Polizia con notizie sulla redazione del Codice Criminale di Malta' (1853) 4 *La Temi: Giornale di Legislazione e di Giurisprudenza*, 681. See also Floriana Colao (2003), 'Il codice di Malta in un «articolo» di Mittermaier per «La Temi» e l'*Avvertenza* di Giuseppe Panattoni' in Sergio Vinciguerra (ed), *Leggi Criminali per l'Isola di Malta e Sue Dipendenze (1854)*, Padua: CEDAM, cxxvii–clv.

disappear.'[106] This caution was necessary, in view of the significant number of differences between the Maltese and the Sicilian Codes.[107]

Had they really severed the umbilical cord, however? Were they, Harlequin-like, accepting the modern idea that a Code is a self-contained instrument while still recognising the ancient tradition of the 'Roman laws'?[108] Was their legal thinking correct, if Masferrer's and Cadoppi's views are right? The Maltese had used the 'Roman law' excuse to resist the imposition of English law in Malta,[109] a proposition strongly pushed[110] by Chief Justice John Stoddart (1773-1856).[111] The British took the Maltese

---

106 The original in Italian reads: 'poiché essendo uno dei caratteri principali de' codici moderni è la perfetta concatenazione di tutte le parti tra se stesse, l'omissione di una minima sanzione del codice Siciliano operata nel progetto, o un cangiamento qualunque introdottovi, può distruggere tutta la sicurezza dell'intelligenza da tali commenti somministrata'. *Rapporto,* xxix.

107 *Ibid.*, xxix.

108 See Harding, 357, 366. See also, Giovanni Garbagnati and Luca Lupária (2007), 'Il processo penale maltese tra modello *adversary* e radici continentali' in Lorenzo Cuocolo and Luca Lupária (eds), *Valori costituzionali e nuove politiche del diritto. Scritti raccolti in occasione del decennale della rivista 'Cahiers Européens'*, Matelica: Halley Editrice, 142.

109 There are many reasons for such an interpretation, including that the legal profession would have had to retrain in law and learn English, but also that the imposition of English law would have meant the total take-over of the Islands' administration by the Power that had to 'protect' and in reality was occupying and colonising. Officially, in England, Lord Glenelg (Secretary of State for War and the Colonies, 18 April 1835-20 February 1839) said that, 'It had certainly been found, that where laws had been transferred from England to Malta, they had occasioned great perplexities and grievous complaints, as the law of bankruptcy, for instance, which, although it was introduced into Malta, yet this was done with a proviso, that nothing in it should derogate from the law of Malta; and the result was, that both laws were in opposition. Trial by jury was also introduced in a law by Sir J Stoddart, but it was found necessary to issue half a dozen other laws to explain and correct it' – (1839) XLVIII *Hansard's Parliamentary Debates Third Series, 2° Victoriæ, 1839* 6, 949-50.

110 Stoddart had originally recommended that a new Criminal Code for Malta be formed 'upon the basis of the English law'. *Ibid.*

111 Stoddart was a journalist and lawyer, who served as editor of *The Times*. He was also the brother-in-law of William Hazlitt. On quite a few occasions, he abused of his position, until his office was finally abolished in the wake of the Austin-Lewis Reports referred to above. Douglas Gourlay (2009), 'Andrew Jameson and the Origins of the Criminal Code of Malta' (2009) 15 (2) *Melita Historica*

seriously on their Roman law claims and, in the early 1840s, called their bluff, as it were, by inviting a young Scottish lawyer virtually unknown outside his native Edinburgh,[112] Andrew Jameson (1811-1870),[113] to revise the 1842 amalgamated Draft Criminal Code and Criminal Procedure Code, on the grounds that Scottish law was, like Maltese law, based on Roman law.[114]

That the British thought the Maltese had been bluffing and that the British called their bluff by inviting a lawyer from another 'Roman law' jurisdiction[115] can be deduced from comments made by Jameson himself:

> Under the Government of the Knights of Malta, the system of Criminal Law and practice was of that severe and arbitrary character which universally prevailed among the Continental Nations until the end of the eighteenth century: and which though attacked by Beccaria and other philosophical Jurists and partially reformed by Leopold of Tuscany, Joseph of Austria and the revolutionary Government of France, has still left many traces in those Countries.[116]

This is not how somebody who hails from a sister neo-Roman-law jurisdiction would write; this is how a lawyer from a common-law jurisdiction would analyse the developments in continental Europe. Strikingly, Jameson's reaction tallies with the line of argumentation used by contemporary legal historians like Masferrer and Cadoppi.

113.

112 This appointment was much to the chagrin of Maltese judge Ignazio Gavino Bonavita, one of the members of the Commission that drafted the Criminal Code.

113 For an enumeration, accompanied by observations and comments, of the correspondence exchanged between the colonial authorities and Jameson on the subject of the revision of the proposed Criminal Code, see Douglas Gourlay (2015), *Sheriff Andrew Jameson: The Life of Effie Gray's Uncle*, Melrose Books, 321-41.

114 See Sammut, 34-35.

115 Da Passano rightly called it *forzatura* (see above). The present author has argued that Scottish Roman law derives from Dutch-Roman law whereas Maltese Roman law from Italian Romano-canonical *ius commune*. See Sammut.

116 Jameson, 10-12.

Of greater interest to us, however, are his remarks on the lingering of the *ius commune* in the Maltese legal system. These remarks are indeed revealing and merit an extraordinary transcription *in extenso*:

> The penal branch of the new Code is closed with a general disposition of great importance, declaring that in all matters not provided for in these Laws, the Laws and particular regulations shall be observed. These reserved Laws include 'the Roman Laws, Customs, the Local Laws of the Island of Malta and its Dependencies, contained in the Municipal Law, *Bandi*, Proclamations and Ordinances and in any other legislative disposition'. [...]

The chief objections to this enactment arise from its dangerous vagueness and generality. Many arbitrary Laws are thus revived which it would be well to consign to oblivion. The learned Commissioners themselves do not know the extent of this provision. If these Laws are known, why are they not enumerated or at least the subjects of them described? If not known or incapable of any description, how unsafe to give them the force of Law without enquiry? In this way, the British Government are made to sanction much of the old legislation, which has been falling into deserved desuetude, without any opportunity of judging either of its nature or extent; and with no means of discovering whether the acts prohibited are either proper offences, or whether the punishments prescribed for them, are just or suitable.

Another objection is, that if any provisions in the penal Code are now suppressed as unnecessary or improper, this will have the strange consequence of reviving some of these prohibitions in a more obnoxious shape: for although they may be expunged from the Code, they will be found either in the Code Rohan, or within the mass of consuetudinary Laws and Ordinances, in a form affording still less precision of description, or fitness of punishment.

The object of this saving clause is said to be, to preserve those special regulations as to the quarantine, customs, police of streets and roads and the like, which must be enforced by penal sanctions, and which at present cannot be revised conveniently, nor abrogated without creating general confusion and disorder.

The object may be quite proper. A similar necessity was felt in the French, Neapolitan and Ionian Codes, but these analogous provisions are not expressed in terms so general as those now proposed. It is thought the general provision goes beyond its object. What have Roman Laws to do with the regulations of police [...]? In preserving what is necessary the provision unfortunately includes much that is absolutely obnoxious.

It is a matter of notoriety that the Roman Laws, not withstanding their deserved celebrity in the matter of civil rights and obligations, contain many objectionable doctrines and arbitrary provisions in respect to crimes; and there are a few enormities in criminal procedure for which the ingenuity of a Civilian may not find authority in the Imperial Rescripts or the Glosses of the Commentators. It will at once occur, what a dangerous latitude is introduced by declaring such a system in force, in matters not regulated by the new Code, even although the punishments applicable by that system are prohibited. The local Laws and Customs of the Island of Malta contained in the *Dritto Municipale, Bandi* and other Ordinances down to the present time, undoubtedly contain many very extraordinary provisions. Many of these and even the Ordinances and Proclamations issued since the British occupation of the Island, were passed for temporary purposes.[117] It seems to be very unsafe to declare this in force to any effect without any thorough revision of the whole. In this way many arbitrary Laws, although unsuitable to the times in which we live, and which have been allowed to fall into tacit oblivion under the administration of British Governors, are in a manner revived; and there is no means of knowing the extent, to which this forgotten mass of contradictory Laws, may be reared up to harass individuals or even obstruct the operation of the new Code.[118]

Jameson, who seems to be echoing Beccaria's pulverisation of the *ius commune*, turns the spotlight on the fact that the *ius commune* seemed to persist in the minds of the Maltese, who, nonetheless, kept protesting that

---

117 Here Jameson was possibly being disingenuous. Indeed, if one looks at the disorderly collection published in 1840 that covers only the years 1784 to 1813, both included, (*Avvertimenti, Collezione di Bandi, Prammatiche ed Altri Avvisi Ufficiali pubblicati dal Governo dell'Isola di Malta e Sue Dipendenze dal 17 Luglio 1784, al 4 Ottobre 1813*), one finds almost two hundred *bandi*. These excluded acts that had transitory and similar matters as their subject-matter.

118 Jameson, 131-33. In this text, Jameson is worried about the British who will be tried under this Code.

they were essentially adapting the French Code to the circumstances of Malta.[119]

The inquisitorial and the accusatorial models

Like other Continental jurisdictions, Malta went through the shift from the *ius commune* to the contemporary legal system to some degree or other. At the same time, being a British possession, Malta also experienced a concurrent shift from the inquisitorial to the accusatorial model.[120] Hence, a quick look at the two models becomes urgently pertinent. To my understanding, the impetus behind the British insistence on introducing their (accusatorial) model in Malta was twofold: the self-serving, conscience-assuaging mantra of the 'enlightened spirit of [the British] Colonial administration' and the privilege bestowed upon the Maltese of enjoying the 'many free institutions of British origin, unknown in the Kingdom of Naples';[121] and, no doubt

---

119 For an overview of Jameson's proposals and their reception by the Maltese, and a brief discussion on the unsurmountable hurdles of mixing Scots law doctrine on murder and manslaughter with the Italian doctrine of homicide, see Cadoppi, cviii-cix and xcix-cv, respectively. Cadoppi's imagery is evocative: the sound of bagpipes is certainly not disagreeable but it would equally certainly jar if it were to accompany *O Sole Mio. Ibid.*, cx.

120 The Ionian Islands (another British 'protectorate' in the Italic sphere) went through a similar experience.

121 Jameson, 4. Jameson's ideas on liberalism call for further scrutiny. Consider his views on the liberal turn in the codification movement, for instance, that triggered the French liberal reform of 1831-1832 and spread throughout Europe. This reform inspired article 62 of the Draft Maltese Criminal Code of 1836, according to which the punishments of the death penalty and perpetual hard labour could be decreased by one degree in case of a valid circumstance extenuating the *dolus*, even if not expressly mentioned by the law as an excuse. Mario Da Passano (2003), 'Le *Leggi Penali* Napoletane e il Primo Progetto di Codice Penale Maltese (1836)', in Sergio Vinciguerra (ed.), *Leggi Criminali per l'Isola di Malta e Sue Dipendenza (1854)*, Padua: CEDAM, lxx. Article 62 was harshly criticised by Jameson who claimed that the introduction of this doctrine 'was considered to be a happy mode of evading the difficulties of the revision of the *Code Napoleon* and the system of punishment, and at the same time of gratifying the popular desire for power' and that 'the practical effect of this doctrine in the proposed Code would be the tacit abolition of capital punishment in all cases. There is a spurious species of humanity prevalent among many classes on the Continent, and very fallacious views are held upon the subject of criminal responsibility which would induce not only Juries but Judge to take advantage of this general privilege of evading the Law in its application to particular cases' – Jameson, 52.

more importantly, the fact that the Code was meant to regulate not only 'the natives of Malta' but also 'a large number of native Englishmen, resident in or resorting to the Island'.[122]

What were the characteristics of the models, and were they really so different? The medieval re-discovery in Italy of Roman law texts ushered in the standardisation of the stages of litigation, witness testimony, and rendering of judgments which, once adopted by the Church, became the 'Romano-canonical procedure'.[123] Later on, the Romano-canonical accusatorial model transitioned to the inquisitorial model, the underlying philosophy of which was that since each crime ultimately causes damage to the *respublica*, the judge was the defender of the interests of the *respublica*; private accusation was thus marginalised, and judges were empowered to initiate criminal proceedings *ex officio*.[124] With the emergence of stronger, centralised, and centralising States, royal legislation increasingly became the main source of law regulating criminal procedure until the seventeenth century, when the Highest Courts (*Grandi Tribunali*) began to make their own rules of procedure[125] which then increasingly acquired the role of non-binding precedent.[126]

---

122 *Ibid.*

123 Schwartz, 341-42. See also K Pennington (2016), 'The Jurisprudence of Procedure' in Wilfrid Hartmann and Kenneth Pennington (eds.), *The History of Courts and Procedure in Medieval Canon Law*, Washington DC: The Catholic University of America Press, 125-59.

124 See Albertus Gandinus (1926 [1460]), *Tractatus de maleficiis*, Berlin: Walter de Gruyter, Vols 1 and 2.

125 Known as *stylus curiae*.

126 See Mario Ascheri (2012), 'Grandi Tribunali Italiani d'età moderna' in *Il contributo italiano alla storia del pensiero – Diritto, Enciclopedia Italiana*; Roy Garré (2009), 'The Dynamics of Law Formation in Italian Legal Science during the Early Modern Period: the Function of Custom' in Wim Blockmans, André Holenstein, and Jon Mathieu (eds), *Empowering Interactions: Political Cultures and the Emergence of the State in Europe 1300-1900*, Abingdon: Ashgate, 93. See also, Gino Gorla (1969), 'I "grandi Tribunali" italiani fra i secoli XVI e XIX: un capitolo incompiuto nella storia politico-giuridica d'Italia' (1969) 92 *Quaderni del Foro italiano* 629–52; Mario Sbriccoli and Antonella Bettoni (eds), (1993), *Grandi tribunali e rote nell'Italia di Antico Regime*, Milan: Giuffré; Rodolfo Savelli (1994), 'Tribunali, "decisiones" e giuristi: una proposta di ritorno alle fonti' in Giorgio Chittolini, Anthony Molho, and Pierangelo Schiera (eds), *Origini dello Stato. Processi di formazione statale in Italia fra medioevo ed età moderna*, Bologna: il Mulino, 397–421.

Some characteristics of the inquisitorial model are worth noting at this stage. It included that the judge initiated *ex officio* proceedings. In the initial stages of the proceedings, the judge heard, in secret, testimonies in support of the accusation. The model further allowed for preventive custody, and examination by the judge of the witnesses.[127] Lawyers for the prosecution and the defence enjoyed a marginal role, while confessions, degree of public knowledge of the crime, and independent testimonies were all accepted as legal proof. Further, torture was used if, despite the examination, doubt still persisted, and sentences were not motivated.

Ironically, if not even paradoxically, Enlightenment thinkers idealised progress but also idealised the conservative Anglo-Saxon accusatorial process. English common law had developed as a virtually autochthonous legal system, separately from the *ius commune*, and it used a technical language and legal notions that were, to a very large extent, incompatible with the language and doctrines of the *Ancien Régime* of continental Europe.[128] On the one hand, the Enlightenment thinkers were dead-set against torture, the presumption of guilt, the secrecy of the acts, and legalisms. On the other hand, they were desirous of importing trial in public, efficacious defence, and verdicts reached by lay juries on the basis on *intime conviction* from England.[129]

In France, the rupture with the *Ancien Régime* dreamt of by the Enlightenment thinkers took place during the French Revolution, prior to which 'old law was good law'. The Enlightenment's confidence in progress altered this belief, such that old law became synonymous with bad law, and as such, had to be abolished. The Revolution did away with the former norms

127 *Istruzione.*

128 Cadoppi, 367.

129 *L'intime conviction* is one of the most important differences between the common law and the continental law approach to evidence today. For the former, the burden of proof lies on the prosecution, and it has to be beyond reasonable doubt. For the latter, the judge is free to evaluate guilt from all evidence adduced, according to his/her conscience (*l'intime conviction*). It was during the eighteenth-century debates of the *Lumières* that the idea was conceived of moral proof, that was later called '*intime conviction*'. There is much historical support for the conclusion that *l'intime conviction* was imported into the Napoleonic Code in 1808 from the English jury system as it existed at the end of the eighteenth century. See Demetra Fr Sorvatzioti and Allan Manson (2019), 'Burden of Proof and *L'intime conviction*: Is the Continental Criminal Trial Moving to the Common Law?' (2019) 23 *Canadian Criminal Law Review* 109–13.

and constitutions and attempted to codify a new law without success. It was Napoleon who succeeded in enacting different codes for the whole of France, not only by introducing new law but also by expressly abrogating all preceding norms, customs, ordinances, and all that had made up the old, variegated legal system now replaced by a monolithic system. Hence the subdivision of French law into pre-revolutionary *ancien droit* and Napoleonic *droit nouveau.*[130]

In England, tradition and uninterrupted continuity prevailed. The common law is the law common to all of England as opposed to local customs;[131] it is timeless and founded on age-old wisdom and its evolution a matter of adjustments, not of radical changes of what, all said and done, is immutable.[132] It is based on the admiration for the judiciary, on the trust reposed in the supremacy of judges as 'makers of the law', and the concomitant aversion toward the legislator as the enabler of developments in the law. It is characterised by the conservative attitude of judges and the attachment to precedents: 'what was good in the past must be good in our own time'.[133]

In reality, no system followed the model in a pure fashion. During the French Revolution, the inquisitorial tradition of the *Ancien Régime* was discontinued when the *Ordonnance criminelle* of 1670 was abrogated. From then onwards, a succession of reforms aimed at importing the English model based on the public trial, oral proceedings, and the jury, culminating in the law of 16-29 September 1791. But the Revolution came to an end in 1799 and was followed by Napoleon and the attempt to strike a balance between the old system and the experiments made during the ten years of the Revolution. Thus, when the French began drafting their new code of criminal procedure, they found two models before them: the inquisitorial of 1670 and the accusatorial of 1791. With the former too backwards and the latter too radical, they decided to combine both, creating a new, mixed

130 RC van Caenegem, 17. The 50 in-between years are known as *droit intermédiare*.

131 *Ibid.*, 22. Pre-Revolution French scholars tried to create a *droit commun français* that would be applicable to all of France and capable of supplanting regional diversity, but failed. Napoleon managed, through his Codes. Ibid.

132 *Ibid.*, 18. However, English legal memory goes back to the coronation of Richard I, on 3 September 1189. Courts do not consider anything prior to that event. Ibid 19.

133 *Ibid.*

system[134] that took shape in the *Code d'instruction criminelle* of 1808 and, two years later, in the Penal Code. Both condensed the old doctrines and the Romano-canonical *regulae juris* into the new spirit of the Enlightenment notion of the Code.[135] The traditional inquisition was retained for the inquiry stage, but the process was invested with the 'character of public, oral, accusatory procedure taking place before a jury, at least for major offen[c]es, and guaranteeing substantial rights to the defen[c]e'.[136] The adaptation of old rules to new philosophies would explain why Napoleon's Penal Code[137] was so readily accepted: it was like a familiar *corpus juris* that incorporated a number of innovations made necessary by historical developments.[138] The Italian penal codes of the Restoration followed the French Code, starting from the Code of the Two Sicilies. This was followed by the Code of Parma (1820), the Gregorian Penal Regulation (1832), the Sardo-Piedmontese Codes (1839 and 1859), and the Code of Este (1855).[139]

Shadow of a shadow?

Jameson believed the Maltese when they argued that they opted for the Code of the Two Sicilies because the proposed Maltese Code was an adaptation of the Sicilian Code (itself 'being no more than the French Code') to the 'circumstances and wants of these Islands'.[140] Yet, he wonders 'whether the laws of France and Naples could be fitted without some modifications to govern a possession of the British Crown' since the French Code contained provisions that 'had been long complained of as a national grievance', and the Neapolitan Code 'was framed for a Country, in which the principles of constitutional government and civil liberty were still less known or appreciated than in France'.[141] Then again, a few paragraphs down, he opines that the proposed Code possessed 'merits of its own, in which, in several particulars, it [wa]s more in harmony with the advanced Jurisprudence and Civilization of the age, than the existing Laws either of France or England'.[142]

134 *Système mixte.*

135 Cadoppi, 366. See Schwartz, 343, 345.

136 Schwartz, 355.

137 And, likewise, his Civil Code.

138 Cadoppi, 366.

139 *Ibid.*, 367.

140 Jameson, 3.

141 *Ibid.*, 3-4.

142 *Ibid.*, 9.

Chief Justice Stoddart[143] , however, had sized up the Draft Criminal Code differently. He had sarcastically dismissed it as a mere 'shadow of the shadow of a Major Planet',[144] that is to say an attenuated version of an attenuated version of something valid.

Accepting Jameson's opinion at face value is a big temptation for any Maltese. The nineteenth century was the century of nationalism, and we therefore have to ask ourselves whether – irrespective of who was right between Stoddart and Jameson – the Maltese Draft mirrors a nascent but growing Maltese legal nationalism expressed in the nationalisation of the criminal law. Jameson passes a telling and striking remark – a sincere remark made by a relatively young man:

> the character, religion and manners of the native population and the habits and education of those who are to administer the Laws, made it an object of importance to preserve as it were the *nationality of the Code*, – in other words, to retain the spirit, system and principles of the Continental Codes as far as possible; because these were more in accordance with the national customs and the ancient Laws, and were upon the whole more suitable to Malta, than any other system.[145]

For Jameson, it seems that tradition and foreign influences are not mutually exclusive.[146] Jameson seems to be accepting the (implied) Maltese

---

143 I have not found much material on Stoddart published in our times, suggesting that he has been forgotten. There is Albert Ganado's short paper [undated] 'Sir John Stoddart (1773-1856)' https://judiciary.mt/en/Documents/bio/Sir%20John%20Stoddart.pdf, accessed 15 October 2021. Ganado states that as Chief Justice of Malta, Stoddart earned 'a salary of £1,500 a year, and [had] a calesse allowance. The six Maltese Judges earned only £428.12s. each'. There is also an accusation of embezzlement or misappropriation (see Giovanni Bonello (2010), 'Pirates in the Early British Era: The Malta Connections' [2010] *Melita Historica* 302); and the question of the abolition of his office (see above). Many satires were written about Stoddart in his day, among which is the tellingly titled *Buonapartephobia: The Origin of Dr. Slop's Name* by William Hone (1820).

144 The original in Italian reads: 'ombra dell'ombra di un Maggior Pianeta'. L De Caro (1845), *Il Processo Criminale in Malta,* Malta: Tipografia Sda Vescovo, 93 fn 2.

145 Jameson, 4-5 [emphasis added].

146 Just like for Masferrer (2018), 20.

argument that categories originating in foreign codes are not necessarily foreign – if the foreign code belongs to the same tradition, then it affords a seamless legal transplant.[147]

Is this a contradiction? It has been argued that the European codes of the nineteenth century 'were the final results of a supranational legal science'.[148] The 'notions, categories, principles and institutions' found in these codes had a validity that was 'supranational and, at the same time – once integrated into the *iura propria* – autochthonous or national'.[149] This apparent paradox requires further investigation with respect to the Maltese Criminal Code.

The nation and the codes

The people living in the times under review – times of transition on many levels – experienced semantic shifts, semantic expansions, and semantic contractions. Consider the word 'nation' itself that oscillated between the older meaning – 'Generations of men born in the same province, or city; § By Birth, Origin, Lineage, Race'[150] – and the modern meaning, that in addition to the two other definitions, includes,

> lineage of men of the same origin and speaking the same language. Union of people bound by civil, moral, intellectual traditions. Society of families in a common and constant bond of descent, traditions, affection, language, institutions, facts, living together. The term nation refers more properly to the situation when men have a common lineage, language, laws, and power, and the will to exercise them.[151]

---

147 This same argument is made by Masferrer (*ibid.*, 21). Masferrer quotes authors both in favour and against the validity of the idea of legal transplants.

148 Masferrer (2016) 107.

149 *Ibid.*, 107 and 115.

150 The original in Italian reads: '*generazion d'uomini nati in una medesima provincia, o città; §. Per Nascimento, Nascita, Origine, Stirpe, Schiatta*'. *Vocabolario dell'Accademia della Crusca* (4th edn 1729-1738) Vol 3, 327. Compare: '*Generazion d'huomini nati in una medesima Provincia, o Città*', repeated in the 3rd edn (1691) vol 3, 1078, 2nd edn (1623) 539; and 1st edn (1612) 552.
Nascimento and *nascita* can both be translated as *birth,* the difference being too subtle for any significant difference in translation.

151 The original in Italian reads: '*schiatta di uomini avente la medesima orig-*

Did the tense arguments between Giandonato Rogadeo and the Maltese jurists in the 1780s centre around a nascent, modern idea of 'nation'? Had they not understood Rogadeo's code as failing to reflect the temperament of the Maltese nation because it was not written by a native who knew the character and spirit of the country?[152] Was it a quarrel about politics (an interpretation obtained if we impose the modern meaning of '*nazione*' on the intention of the *dramatis personae*) or about law (an interpretation reached if we use the former meaning of '*nazione*', ie, the meaning that was still current at the time of the quarrel)?[153] In this period, it seems Maltese jurists understood 'nation' as the subject of a *ius proprium*,[154] ie, part of the *Ancien Régime* system, not as the subject of a national(ised) legal system, ie, the hallmark of the modern liberal/constitutional system. The intellectual journey towards the modern concept of 'nation' had still to be undertaken, and the role the criminal law was to play in it was still in the making. Then again, the late-eighteenth-century Maltese were alive to the concept slowly expanding in the universe of ideas, as can be seen from the fact that they were quarrelling with Rogadeo exactly on the lines of the twin tensions compressed in the concept: tradition and foreign influences.

If we follow Masferrer, there is a 'dichotomy between tradition and foreign influences' in the criminal codes.[155] The school of thought for which the codes broke scientifically with the past tends to place too much emphasis

ine e parlante la lingua medesima. Unione di gente in vincolo di tradizioni civili, morali, intellettuali. Società di famiglie in vincolo comune e costante di discendenza, di tradizioni, d'affetti, di linguaggio, d'istituzione, di fatti, d'abitazione. Quella é più propriamente nazione, ove gli uomini hanno comune la schiatta, la lingua, le leggi, e la potenza, e la volontà d'eserguirle'. Tommaseo-Bellini (1869), *Nuovo Dizionario della Lingua Italiana*, Turin: UTET, Vol 3, Part 1, 451.
The latter dictionary warns that, 'the indeterminately promiscuous meanings that we give to People, People, Nation, are a historical document to be meditated upon, on which to make a chemical analysis to distinguish its possible elements'. Ibid.

152 Muscat, 72, 93, 125.

153 For an interpretation with a different nuance, see Frans Ciappara (2006), *Enlightenment and Reform in Malta 1740- 1798*, Malta: Midsea Books, 66-67.

154 The legal system of the *Ancien Régime* had multiple legal sources. It included a Europe-wide *ius commune* (where the 'jurist and criminal lawyer belong[ed] to all countries and [was] an authority in all' (Ortolan [1841], *Cours de Législation Pénale Comparée*, cited by Schwartz, 342) in which 'case law and especially doctrine were […] of an international character' (ibid). It further included local laws, known as *iura propria*.

155 Masferrer (2018), 19.

on foreign influences on the criminal codes. The school that argues that the codes continued many traditional institutes tends to underrate the impact of foreign influences.[156] Masferrer argues that in assessing a code, one has to understand whether it entailed a nationalisation or a denationalisation of its criminal law.[157] Further research is required to determine whether (i) by adapting the Codes that inspired it, the Draft Criminal Code nationalised Maltese criminal law; or (ii) by following dominant European models, it denationalised that law; or (iii) it confirmed what some scholars have argued, namely that codification was a means to both nationalise and denationalise European legal traditions. This last proposition seems to be a paradox. On the one hand, the fact that laws needed to be approved by national parliaments and that the *ius commune* – which was somehow regarded as a foreign law – ceased to be in force points to how much codification contributed to the nationalisation of law. On the other hand, the fact that national parliaments enacted codes, the content of which had been highly influenced by foreign codes, indicates that codification also contributed to the denationalisation of law. Ultimately, the paradox could be resolved by accepting the two processes (adaptation of foreign Codes and following dominant models) as subcontraries.

Where were the Maltese on the graph depicting the growth of the embracing of the 'nation' (y-axis) across time (x-axis)? As strange as it may sound, the answer might be found in the sort of respectful manner with which the British seem to have treated the Maltese *élite* at this time. The British could have resorted to more force, but they did not. It must have occurred to the British, at least in those early years of the occupation, that they had taken over a European Principality run by a native upper class that, though Catholic,[158] was sophisticated: Italian by language, French by culture, and made up the *élite* of a self-aware 'nation'.[159] Then again, were the British guided by the ideology as expressed by GF Leckie – 'while France

---

156 *Ibid.*

157 *Ibid.*

158 The British held disparaging opinions on Catholics in general. Jameson's Report, say, offers many examples, despite the passing in 1829 of the Roman Catholic Relief Act, also known as the Catholic Emancipation Act.

159 Victor Mallia-Milanes, Professor of History at the University of Malta, explains this 'Gallicization' persuasively. See Victor Mallia-Milanes (1988), 'The Genesis of Maltese Nationalism' in Victor Mallia-Milanes (ed), *The British Colonial Experience 1800-1964: The Impact on Maltese Society*, Malta: Mireva, 6.

conquers to devastate, Britain conquers to do good'[160] – or did they retain the memory of the ruthlessness with which the Maltese rural populace had 'butchered' the French during the 1798-1800 insurrection?[161]

The Maltese of the Capital City[162] appear to have been a unique species. They exhibited the cultural dividends acquired over long years spent sharing the Capital City's minuscule surface area with the younger members of the most prestigious noble families of Europe who spent lavish money on the Islands, building monumental defence structures and palatial mansions like maniacs, and took monastic orders yet lived like overgrown naughty teenagers, even procreating with the Maltese. The British must have been in awe of the population of this conurbation – it is tempting to think that there can be no other rational explanation not only for what seems, at least in the context of the codification of criminal law, as decency but also for their insistence on respecting 'public opinion'.[163]

It seems evident that, despite the paradoxical nature of the ideological relationship between the code and the 'nation', the Maltese followed the European *Zeitgeist* of their time and – wittingly or unwittingly – were

160 Quoted by Rosselli, 117.

161 On one occasion, 'the furious mood of the villagers was raised to a higher pitch by a few shots from the garrison that had already decided to surrender. The garrison was butchered, their bodies burned "on a nearby hill". Other French sympathisers [...] met the same fate' – V Mallia-Milanes (1988), 10. The British ingratiated themselves with the local Church, having quickly grasped the all-important notion that the clergy commanded the rural population – after all, a clergyman, Francesco Saverio Caruana, had been one of the generals of the Maltese during the insurrection against the powerful French.

162 Valletta, Birgu, and Senglea were 'composite parts of a whole, collectively constituting the capital city of Malta'. Victor Mallia-Milanes (2019), 'Valletta: Malta's Hospitaller City. An Epitome of Europe' in Victor Mallia-Milanes, *Valletta: Malta's Hospitaller City and Other Essays*, Malta: Midsea Books, 15.

163 Or else, it was only a matter of expediency. A cooperative and docile population needed less money and less resources to administer than a hostile one (as the French learnt during their two years on the Island, and the Germans would learn elsewhere during World War II). Furthermore, at least one colonial administrator, Sir W Reid (Governor of Malta 1851-1858), was convinced that 'in the event of a war with a foreign power the defence of Malta would require the cordial aid of the Maltese people' and that 'their support would be readily given if Britain refrained from opposing their wishes on questions such as the revised Criminal Code' – Hilda I Lee (2017), *Constitutional History of Malta 1800-1914*, UK: Whitelocke Publications, 175.

building their tiny nation like the other Europeans were building theirs, also through the codification of the criminal law.

Conclusion

This article has tried to analyse the intellectual milieu in which the Maltese Criminal Code came into being. It has also cast a glance at the tensions between the Maltese and the possibly benevolent British during the troubled journey that led to the promulgation of the Criminal Code in 1854, with tentative extrapolations on nation-building.

The Maltese were living in times of transition that are challenging for the legal historian to interpret. There was not only the Europe-wide shift from the *Ancien Régime* to a modernity that constantly strove to strike a balance between liberalism and traditionalism. There was also an added uncertainty in Malta engendered by the fact that the new British overlords belonged to a legal tradition that apparently stood outside the continental system where those liberal-traditionalist tugs-of-war were taking place. The Maltese drafters of the Criminal Code seem to have thought like typical Europeans: they handled the old legal principles in the light of the new Enlightenment philosophy. At the same time, however, they had to contend with the added stress of having to accommodate the colonial master and his legal system. Yet, when they looked closely at that system, they seem to have spotted what was probably clear to every well-read lawyer of the time: all in all, the English and the Continental systems were not as disparate as to lie beyond the Maltese ability to conciliate.[164]

---

[164] See Garbagnati and Lupária, 142.

Common Law Contributions to the Maltese Rendition of the French Penal Code: Preliminary Observations

Paper presented at the Fifth Worldwide Congress of the
World Society of Mixed Jurisdiction Jurists
June 14-16 2023
hosted by the
Faculty of Law, University of Malta

A dispute broke out in June 1838 between Britain and Naples on the sulphur mining monopoly in Sicily. The King of the Two Sicilies aimed to remove the British merchants from his kingdom, and thus granted the monopoly to the French company *Taix Aycard & C.* [1] The dispute, resolved in 1840, obviously drew the attention of the British press that kept targeting the king of the Two Sicilies and France.[2] It should not surprise the observer that the Two Sicilies and France were on people's minds in Malta. Malta was for centuries historically defined, at least in part, by Sicily (and Naples) and France: by the Two Sicilies on account of geographical proximity, by France because, as Alain Blondy has repeatedly pointed out, many within Malta's elite were Franco-Italian. The range of this impact included the legal sphere.

In his *Il Processo Criminale di Malta* (1845), de Caro quotes Chief Justice (and former journalist) John Stoddart's sarcastic dismissal of the draft Maltese Criminal Code as "*ombra dell'ombra di un Maggior Pianeta*" – the shadow of a shadow of a Major Planet. For indeed, what the title refers to as the Maltese Rendition of the French Penal Code – that is to say, what would later become the Criminal Code of Malta – was inspired by the Code for the Kingdom of the Two Sicilies of 1819, itself modelled on the French Code.

Inspired, that is, with some additions. This essay will be looking at the inspiration and the additions, closing by zeroing in on the two types of common-law contributions.

The Sicilian Code

For the purposes of this essay, "Sicilian" refers to the Two Sicilies, Sicily and Naples. The name of the Code too requires clarification: the Sicilian Code was not simply a Penal Code. It was subdivided into five parts, the second of which dealt with penal laws while the other four with civil and commercial law, and civil and criminal procedure. The main objective of the Code – i.e., of the five parts taken together – was to have, to quote Alfonso Stile, an "entire *corpus* of national law that was adapted to the nature of the peoples it was addressed to, in their current state of civilisation and that

1 Alessia Facineroso (2010), "The Sicilian Revolution of 1848 as seen from Malta", *Symposia Melitensia* No. 6, 36–42, 37.

2 *Ibid.*

encompassed the important objective of the safety of persons and property".[3] This was the philosophy of the Sicilian Code.

The second part of the Sicilian Code was heavily influenced by the *code pénal*, the Penal Code of the French. This could not have been otherwise, as the French Code was in force in the peninsular part of the Kingdom of the Two Sicilies from October 1, 1812 until it was replaced by when the Neapolitan Code (or the Code of the Two Sicilies) in August 1819.

The Two Sicilies drafters allowed themselves to be influenced by the French Code, but also introduced their own original ideas. However, their Code also reflected the politics prevailing in their Kingdom at the time: the intertwining of Religion and Politics was the bedrock on which the absolute and confessional Monarchy was built.

This was the Code that inspired the Maltese drafters: the French Penal Code refracted through the prism of the Two Sicilies. The Sicilian penal laws, however, did not exist as a stand-alone Code; they formed part of a larger Code that incorporated the five main subdivisions of the law (Civil, Commercial, Penal, Civil Procedure and Criminal Procedure) and that reflected the spirit of the times, when parts of Europe were going through the process whereby the capitalist class acquired political dominance. Private property attained paramount importance. Common lands – on which different categories of people had different rights, ranging from ownership to enjoyment – ceased to be common: land was privatised. A new philosophy ascended to political dominance: private ownership would ensure the highest level of exploitation of land; moreover, free trade, including free trade of land, would help attain this economic growth. This new *liberal* philosophy – the freedom to trade and the freedom to own in an exclusive fashion, free of the rights of others – was forged in the furnace of the French Revolution (1789 to 1799) and gained momentum during the Restoration. The freedom to own and trade land, to cultivate it in a new, industrialised fashion, and the contemporary industrial revolution, needed a new way of thinking: a new mental, but also political, constitution. The new political constitution meant restrictions on the powers

---

3 *'un intero corpo di diritto patrio che fosse adatto all'indole dei nostri popoli, allo odierno stato della civilizzazione e che rachiudesse il grande oggetto della sicurezza delle persone e della proprietà'*, from *Collezione leggi e decreti del Regno delle due Sicilie* 1815, quoted in Alfonso Stile (1993), 'Il codice penale del 1819 per lo Regno delle due Sicilie' in Sergio Vinciguerra, *I Codici Preunitari e il Codice Zanardelli*, Padua: CEDAM, 188.

of the State permitting the unfettered freedom to trade, to own, to exploit – to be left in peace in order to do (*laissez-faire*). This new political direction needed a shift in legal philosophy and the codes became implements of the new, constitutional thinking. In the new philosophy, the Civil Code was meant to protect and regulate the land owners' and capitalists' rights of ownership, enjoyment, and exploitation, while the Criminal Code was meant to keep the others, those who were neither capitalists nor land-owners, in check. Not only in order to avoid that these others would steal, but also to ensure that they would not revolt against the new order. Though the French did not enact the five Codes together, their five Codes were legal emanations of the same political philosophy. The Two Sicilies took what was most probably the next logical step, enacting the five laws as subdivisions of the same Code, underlying the philosophical unity between them as different facets of the same political setup based on economic relations and the dominant economic framework.

The Maltese Code

This philosophical unity was missing in Malta. The Criminal Code came into existence almost as if it existed in a world different from that regulated by the yet-to-be-promulgated Civil and Commercial Codes. It is suggested that this was due to three reasons.

First, the small surface area of the Maltese archipelago rendered unthinkable the application of the economic theories underlying the political push on the continent to privatise land ownership.

The second reason is possibly that neither the French (during the two years they occupied Malta – as argued by Alain Blondy) nor the British (as argued by Mario Vella) were interested in creating, or even permitting the creation of, a Maltese capitalist class. One would tend to subscribe to the theory, expounded mostly by Mario Vella in his *Reflections in a Canvas Bag* when he writes about the attempts made in Naples and Malta in the last years of the eighteenth century to create "anti-feudal revolutions". Vella argues that

> the consequence of [those] failed bourgeois revolutions [...] was a regional restoration (in which the British Royal Navy played from the very outset a not insignificant role) that, on the one hand, retarded

> the autonomous development of the ideological, economic and political conditions necessary for the development of modern manufacturing capitalism and, on the other hand, artificially propped up formations characterised by pre-capitalist relations of production in the countryside and parasitic merchant capital in the urban centres.[4]

Vella argues that "[t]his ideological, economic and political stagnation lasted at least until the second world war."[5] Without a local capitalist class, the philosophy underlying the liberal constitutionalism of Restoration Europe would not make sense in nineteenth-century Malta.

The third and last reason is possibly what has been termed, by Aniceto Masferrer, as British "Codiphobia."[6] Masferrer argues that there was more passion than science in the common lawyers' resistance to codification. Be that as it may, the fact remains that, despite the Penal Code for India, the common law – at least in the nineteenth century – had very little enthusiasm for codification. That said, here codification is intended more in the philosophical, than the strictly legislative, sense – that is to say, codification as an emanation of the legal philosophy needed to put into place and into practice the economic model wanted and pushed by the emerging continental capitalist class, not simply codification in the sense of collecting in one book the rules regulating a particular segment of the law. The British capitalist class managed to achieve its aims without the need for a continental-style code, possibly thanks to the flexibility afforded by the case-by-case approach of the common law system that starts off from the practical case rather than from theoretical rules.

So whereas the Maltese draft Criminal Code owes its substantive contents mostly to the French model filtered through the Two Sicilies prism, the political context it came into being in was different from that of the Two Sicilies, because Malta was a British colony. The nature of the Code depends on the context in which it is engendered – the content ultimately depends on the context in which it is framed. The French approach was to

---

4 Mario Vella (1989), *Reflections in a Canvas Bag: Beginning philosophy between politics and history*, Malta: PEG, 173.

5 *Ibid.*

6 Aniceto Masferrer (2019), 'French Codification and "Codiphobia" in Common Law Traditions', 34 *The Tulane European and Civil Law Forum*, 1–31.

consider the five subdivisions of the law – the five codes – as implements of the liberal constitution; English eyes saw these codes as "monsters".[7] Furthermore, there was the common-law aversion to the top-down approach, the approach of the written liberal Constitutions of Continental Europe and their extensions, the written, philosophically-unified Codes. This is possibly the third reason why the Maltese Criminal Code is philosophically different to its French-Sicilian model.

Unconscious contribution

This would also be the first Common Law contribution to the Maltese Criminal Code, arguably an unconscious contribution and an interpretation buttressed by the fact that both the Civil and the Commercial Codes of Malta did not appear at the same time as the Criminal Code, but later, and piecemeal, as Ordinances. The overarching philosophical approach that characterised the French (and Sicilian) model was completely lacking in Malta, because of the British matrix in which these codes came into being.

It could be argued that the policy of delay embraced by the British administration with regard to the conclusion of the process of drafting the Criminal Code of Malta can be explained, at least in part, by this mentality.

The Scottish connection

On a more conscious level, the Common Law contributions in the nineteenth century include for sure the assignment with which Scottish lawyer Andrew Jameson was tasked.

The Maltese repeatedly insisted with the British colonial administration that the Maltese legal tradition was essentially Roman (which was more or less correct) and that therefore they could not import English Common Law. A Royal Commission in 1812 agreed with them, 'deprecat[ing] the total abrogation of the existing laws as a measure neither desired nor desirable. [...] In the case of Malta they thought it would be found more expedient to adapt the remedies to the growth which the tree had taken than to apply the hatchet

---

7 See F.H. Lawson (1977), *Many Laws*, North-Holland Publishing Company, 48. There are of course practical issues involved in codification in common law system – see, Peter M. North (1982), 'Problems of Codification in a Common Law System', *Rabels Zeitschrift für ausländisches und internationales Privatrecht / The Rabel Journal of Comparative and International Private Law*, 1982, 46. Jahrg., H. 3, 490-508.

to the root."[8] This notwithstanding, intent on establishing the common law for criminal matters in Malta, the colonial administration identified an intelligent solution: a Scottish lawyer would be brought over to bridge the gap between the traditional native legal system and the legal system of the colonial masters – Scots law too, or so it was claimed, derived from Roman law.

Little did it matter that the Roman pedigree of Scots law was a myth – by the beginning of the nineteenth century the Scots had long stopped going to the Netherlands for their education, and had instead started forming themselves in London. But even before that, even when the Scots still went to the Netherlands to study law, Scots law was not a direct descendant of Roman Law; it was influenced by Dutch-Roman law, that is to say Dutch law as expressed in Roman terms.[9] The connection of Maltese law to Roman Law, on the other hand, was more intimate: it was 'with Roman, Canon, and Sicilian law, the reforms and the new case-law, and the customs and usages of the Courts'.[10] But political expediency made such niceties redundant. The Maltese claimed that they belonged to the Roman law tradition, so did the Scots, and it was therefore logical for the colonial administration to invite a Scotsman to prune the Maltese draft Criminal Code with a view to making it more palatable to the common-law masters. In reality, however, as Cadoppi convincingly argues, already in the nineteenth century, Scots lawyers were as common-law as their English counterparts, despite their persistent Roman law mythology.

Andrew Jameson

The Scottish lawyer in question was Andrew Jameson.[11]

If one looks into Jameson's Report, published in 1844, with the eye of the historian more than that of the lawyer, one finds that the Scottish lawyer brought with him a lot of Protestant prejudice against Catholics, and particularly against Southern Europeans, considered to be sexually

---

8 Hugh W. Harding (1968), *Maltese Legal History Under British Rule (1801-1836)*, Malta: The Author, 63.

9 See Mark A. Sammut (2017), 'Historical Facts and Myths surrounding the Criminal Code of Malta', in Mark A. Sammut, *Essays in Maltese Legal History and Comparative Law*, Oxford: OLP.

10 Antonio Micallef, *col dritto romano – canonico – e siculo – le riforme e la nuova giurisprudenza – le consuetudini e gli usi dei Tribunali.*

11 See Sammut, *op. cit.*

lax, temperamentally rash, and, all in all, unable to overcome the different temptations of the flesh and of their unreformed (and therefore primitive) religion. As a matter of fact, this prejudice acquires constitutional relevance: it re-surfaces in Rapinet's constitutional law lectures, but this time internalised by the colonised:

> In territories acquired by conquest or cession, the existing laws and customs of the people are retained until the native population becomes qualified to share the franchises of Englishmen, which are gradually introduced. In territories however of the latter description, held only as garrison towns or naval stations, or else peopled by races hostile to the British rule, or unfit for freedom, the government is based on different principles, and only such English institutions and rights are granted, which are compatible with the security of the Colony and with imperial interests.[12]

The legal historian, however, will find Jameson's report valuable because it betrays a mix of diverse legal elements. For instance, the Maltese drafters borrowed an English provision on "barratry" (abuses by lawyers) which did not exist in either the French or the Sicilian Code – Jameson criticises them and argues that that provision should be left out because it had fallen into 'deserved desuetude'.

In another instance, Jameson insists that the Maltese Code should criminalise incest and bestiality. For the Maltese mind, moulded by Catholicism, these behaviours belonged to morality not to the law – whereas for the Puritan mind, the law cannot be extricated from morality. It is perhaps ironic, at least up to a point, that bestiality was made a crime only recently (the same year it was criminalised in France), so many decades after independence, even though not through an amendment to the Criminal Code but to the Animal Welfare Act.

But let us consider a couple of other examples from Jameson's report. The Maltese Draft followed the Sicilian Code in reducing the punishment for the rape of a prostitute. Jameson points out that the Sicilian law was inspired

---

12 G. Rapinet (1883), *Lectures on the British Constitution and on the Government of Malta*, Malta: A. Aquilina, 136.

by Gaetano Filangieri's ideas, but that the Laws of England, Scotland, the United States and even France, made allowance for no such reduction. It would seem that the Maltese Code as promulgated in 1854 left this reduction in punishment out.

Following the French (and Belgian) model, the Maltese draft Code introduced offences relating to the arts, manufacture, and copyright. Jameson reacts: 'No such offence is known in the Criminal Law of England and when the subject was lately considered in Parliament it was not found necessary to enforce these rights by way of Criminal process.'[13] But, he then argues that 'if it is thought proper that the chapter should be retained, the provisions would require to be revised, so as to render the duration of the right, the same as in other parts of the Empire'. The Code as promulgated in 1854 does not contain any offence relating to the arts, manufacture and copyright. One wonders whether this was already in line with the colonial policy of deliberately keeping native capitalism in the colonies in a perpetual state of underdevelopment.[14]

(For completeness' sake, it must be pointed out that there were elements in the Maltese draft Code deriving from German legal thinking, such as the theory of instantaneous passion as an excuse to reduce criminal responsibility.)

Throughout Jameson's Report, we find a constant anxiety related to different punishments for the same facts constituting an offence under both English and Maltese law. The tendency in the Report is to suggest that the Maltese punishment be identical to the punishment under English law.

Conclusion

In conclusion, my preliminary observations on this topic are that there were unconscious influences and conscious influences. Despite the obvious racial prejudices – one reads in Jameson's Report recurrent references to the 'Southern European race' – the British did their best to accommodate Maltese sentiment, while trying to keep the law applicable in Malta as acceptable as possible to British people living in the colony. This partly conscious,

---

13 Andrew Jameson (1844), *Report on the Proposed Code of Criminal Laws for the Island of Malta and its Dependencies*, Malta, 106.

14 See Onur Ulas Ince (2020), *Colonial capitalism and the dilemmas of liberalism*, Oxford: Oxford University Press, *passim*.

partly unconscious balancing act – meant to lighten the colonial burden as much as possible – has, at least in part, given rise, in my view, to the hybrid nature of Maltese criminal law. Furthermore, whereas the development of the criminal law in other European territories was meant to pave the way for the consolidation of the political and economic power of the nascent capitalist and industrialist class, in Malta the criminal law seems to have developed to serve the objectives of the colonial power – namely, to reduce tensions with the natives while consolidating the structures of imperialism that would benefit the Mother Country. I would argue that this holds true for at least some decades of the colonial experience – certainly, however, with regard to post-Independence Malta, further inputs from the Common Law came through the psychological process described by Martti Koskenniemi in his *The Gentle Civilizer of Nations* (Cambridge University Press, 2001), whereby the formerly colonised decide spontaneously and out of their free will to copy the former coloniser. Maltese theorist of memory studies Charles Xuereb has compared it to the Stockholm Syndrome.[15]

---

[15] Charles Xuereb (2015), 'Malta Stockholm Syndrome (or why we love the British)', 13 THINK Magazine, 48–55.

CONSTITUTIONAL HISTORY

Amabile Bonello's
Essay on the Public Law of Malta

Appeared in *Id-Dritt Law Journal* Vol. XXX (2020)

In 1868, Amabile Bonello published an essay called *Diritto Pubblico di Malta,* 'The Public Law of Malta'. In Bonello's essay, the legal theory is more implicit than explicit. Even though Bonello himself claims that his 'little work' was the first Maltese treatise on Public Law,[1] it is, in fact, the attempt of a layman to discuss the Constitutional law of his homeland, not for the formulation of a legal theory as much as for the formulation of political reasons to back one of the numerous requests made to London, the Empire's Metropolis, for self-government. But as in Constitutional law there is no clear-cut line of demarcation between political history (convention, description, 'wisdom of the ages') and abstract legal thinking (statute law, prescription, 'artificial reason of law'), this essay is fascinating for the legal historian.

For the political historian, the interest lies in the very fact that the essay was written. The text, or so it seems to the present author, was meant to hearten the Maltese, the implication being that there was only lukewarm support for constitutional reform.

This study's objectives are to offer a translation of Bonello's essay[2] as well as some background to both author and essay. As far as I can establish, this will be the first time that a translation of this essay is being published.

Translation

> *When there is a serious case in which positively a private benefit must or can be sacrificed in favour of a public benefit, then it is necessary to recall the good family man, who frugally has his grain ground and removes something from the bread that he gives to his family, in order to save the seeds for the coming year, to avoid that they go through the horrors of hunger. Unfortunately, it is the sacrifice of a real but smaller need of particular individuals, which out of necessity is done for their better need.*
>
> – Romagnosi

1 *'... il mio desio di delineare i contorni del nostro Diritto Publbico ... sul quale non comparve ancora nessuno trattato'* – Amabile Bonello (1868), *Diritto Pubblico di Malta,* Malta: Tipografia del *Portafoglio Maltese,* 21.

2 The translation is of the present author, save where other texts are quoted and the present author managed to find contemporary translations of them.

My homeland was never deprived of that self-government that accomplishes Public law. — Already under the Romans, the Maltese were administered by their own magistrates and their own laws. After the vicissitudes under the Vandals and the Saracens, the latter being ousted by Count Roger, he gave back to the Maltese their freedoms.[3] Then followed a union with Sicily and Naples that took various forms. Following some changes, Ludwig King of Aragon and Sicily united Malta to Sicily on the 2 October 1350, giving Malta its self-government. In 1426, when King Alfonso gave Malta as security to the Monroy family for the 30,000 florins he owed them, the Maltese paid this sum on the condition that these Islands should never again be alienated. By means of a royal diploma of 20 June 1428, the King bound himself not to alienate this land, and to uphold its freedoms, adding that if his successors failed to observe this agreement, then the Maltese were freed from their oath of fealty and could oppose the King's illegal acts through the use of force, without being held responsible for the crime of *fellonia*. The main freedoms were: 1. That the Maltese not be summoned for litigation out of their islands; that commissioners not be sent for civil and criminal cases; that the Maltese be exempt from paying taxes to Sicily; that citizens vote to elect holders of public office; that the *capitano*[4] and the jurats[5] be obliged to obey the resolutions of the Popular Council;[6] that the same person not occupy more than one public office; furthermore, that the Maltese have the right to send two deputies to the Parliament in Sicily, as attached to the Kingdom.

2. My forefathers always had the Popular Council, known as *Universitas*, that represented the entire population and managed the affairs of the country, decreed taxes, reduced them, regulated their distribution, decreed the rules regulating commerce, oversaw and censured holders of public office, sent ambassadors even to different Sovereigns.

3. When the population learnt that the Island would be ceded to the Hierosolymitan Order, the Council met on 10 April 1524 and decreed that the magnificent[7] Giacomo Angarao de Inguanez and Alvarao de Casseres be sent

---

3 *'Freedoms'* (or *'exceptions'*) not *'privileges'* as Bonello uses *'franchigie'* not *'privilegi'*, even though he probably meant *'privileges'*.

4 The *Capitano della Verga* was the Governor of the Islands, the *Ħakem*.

5 Or *giurati*, the elected judges.

6 Or *Consiglio popolare*; it administered the islands.

7 "Magnificent" might sound hyperbolic, if not even pompous. However, the

as ambassadors to the Viceroy and then to the Emperor, to examine the form of the concession and, should it be found to derogate from the homeland's freedom, to obtain a different one or else contest it. During the Council of 16 May 1530, the Council debated the form of the oath to the Grand Master, laying down that if the Religion should leave the Island, the Island would return to the Crown. The following were present: the Magnificent Leonardo Calava chief of the city, the nobles Vassallo, Xerri, Zammit, Callus, Xeberras, Cumbo, etc, etc, and the representatives of the casals,[8] notably *De Cappella* (that is from the Casal Naxaro) Francesco Muscat, Antonio Tinense, and Gio. Micallef, De Cappella Birchircara, Lorenzo Zammit, and Gio. Mansun, etc, etc. It was concluded that the oath be taken by the *capitano* and the jurats on behalf of all the inhabitants. When the Order's commissioners arrived to take possession of the country, the jurats did not take the oath in the name of the people, until the commissioners had[9] vowed in the name of the Order to observe all their privileges[10] in the future. But even after this, the *Universitas* sent Ambassadors to Syracuse (where the Order had settled at that time) for the ratification of said stipulation and the Grand Master and his entire Council ratified the procedure of their commissioners and vowed strictly to respect the privileges.

4. Following this agreement, the Order took over Malta, and each Grand Master took possession of the former capital city in the name of the people, having first vowed to respect all the privileges that the Maltese enjoyed since the time of the Aragonese kings. And even though the Religion did not really religiously observe the word given, the freedoms were evidently not abrogated, and the councils were convoked on numerous occasions. Let us mention the council meeting of 20 January 1591, which decreed that, since the Viceroy had not sent grain, then all the grain found in the harbour was to be bought, and then sold at a moderate price to the people. This demonstrates that at the time of my forefathers, the representatives of the people exercised

notion of magnificence goes back to Classical Antiquity and was used throughout the Middle Ages and the Renaissance, up until the 18th century, and refers to the greatness of actions, bravery, honour, generosity, and noble purposes.

8 "Casals" is the term used by Samuel Taylor Coleridge – see Barbara E. Rooke (ed.) (1969), *The Collected Works of Samuel Taylor Coleridge: The Friend*, Vol 4, Part II, Routledge & Kegan Paul Ltd, London/Princeton University Press, Princeton NJ, 360.

9 The flow of the text suggests that here the author meant '*avessero*' not the word which he actually used, namely '*abbiano*'.

10 Here the author uses '*privilegi*' not '*franchigie*'.

the sublime right and majestic[11] obligation to provide for the needs of the public.

5. *Municipal affairs*, even under the Order's rule, were administered by both the jurats and the *Universitas*, both directly and indirectly through the holders of public office. The jurats of Mdina governed the City, managed the Hospital, etc, and had jurisdiction over various cases belonging to their office, as well as the right to decide at appellate stage the civil cases appealed from the *Curiæ Capitanalis*. The *Universitas* of Valletta took care of the oil, coal, meat, and grain, maintaining the prices moderate even if on the free market they were costlier; cleaned and illuminated the streets; oversaw the cleanliness of the markets, the fair weight, etc, through jurats and subordinates to whom it paid a salary; provided supplies and other necessities to the Hospices and prisons, etc. Succinctly put, it had all the attributes of a municipality. There was a similar magistracy on Gozo. The last jurats of the Capital were Dr Giuseppe Bonnici, Alessandro Patrizio Spiteri, Leopoldo Zahra Glinchan,[12] and Dr Giuseppe Muscat. This magistracy and Valletta's were abrogated in 1818.

6. When the Island was ceded to the French Republic with the Convention signed on 12 June 1798, Article 7 of said Convention expressly laid down that the Maltese *'will conserve the belongings and privileges they possess'*. And yet the Maltese, unhappy with the measures taken against their rights by the French, organised the general revolt of the countryside on the 2 September 1798 and two days later, that is on the 4 September, re-established the *Popular Council*, composed of the generals, the battalion chiefs, and the *representatives of the people elected by all the heads of family*. The entire country was governed by that Council, save for Valletta and the three maritime Cities. That Council established and controlled the taxes, appointed deputies for public health, interned on Comino the wrongdoers and those suspected of collaborating with the French, ordered a national loan, appointed customs officers, took measures for provisions, authorised the representatives to collect monies whereby poor women could be supplied with spinning wheels, etc – in brief, it managed all the affairs of the Island.

In the meantime, the Maltese defeated the French sorties and

---

11 In the sense of "(belonging to the) sovereign".

12 According to the Baron Azopardi, the surname is 'Zahra Clinchant' – see, Baron Azopardi (1843), *Raccolta di Varie Cose Antiche e Moderne Utili ed Interessanti Riguardanti Malta e Gozo*, Malta, 96.

blockaded the fortifications from the land side. A few English and Neapolitan troops arrived, together with Portuguese and English vessels to blockade the fortifications from the sea side. The forts then capitulated and when the English and the Neapolitans occupied Valletta, it was agreed that the ancient freedoms[13] and laws of Malta would be preserved (Sir A.J. Ball's letter to William Winsham, Secretary of State, 28 February 1807). Furthermore, General Pigot published in February 1801 a proclamation whereby he declared himself to be the *representative of His Britannic Majesty on Malta and Gozo* and assured the Maltese Nation of the King's protection and the *full possession of its Religion, its property, and its Liberty*. The Royal Commissioner Charles Cameron[14] in his proclamation of 15 July 1801, addressed the following words to the Maltese Nation: 'Charged by His Majesty, the King of Great Britain, to conduct all the affairs (except the military) of these islands, I embrace with the highest satisfaction, this opportunity of assuring you that His Majesty grants you full protection, and the enjoyment of your dearest rights'.[15]

News reached Malta of the Treaty of Amiens, according to which the Order had once again to take possession of Malta; a congress was held on the 9 November 1801 that elected a deputation to bring to the fore the opposition of the Maltese and their wish to remain united with Great Britain. The representatives, though elected by all the heads of family, considered that they could not carry out an act of such importance without the *consent of the entire people*. Consequently, they issued this *Notice*: 'The lieutenants of the Governor and the Representatives of the people have deputised the Marquis Don Mario Testaferrata, Filippo Castagna, Emanuele Ricaud, Don Pietro Mallia, and Michele Cachia to travel to London and inform His Majesty of the situation... etc. Such a deputation is of interest to the entire Nation, and the said Representatives wish that it be approved by the entire Nation. Thus, these presents are meant to give notice of it to all, so that whosoever intends to oppose it should within three days hand any representation to the Notary of the Curiæ Capitanalis of Mdina if from the countryside, and as regards the four Cities to the Notaries of the Grand Court of Valletta.

---

13 Or *'privileges'*.

14 *Royal* Commissioner is the term used by Bonello: '*Commissario Regio*'; Cameron was Royal Civil Commissioner.

15 This part would seem to paraphrase the line of argument found in Giorgio Mitrovich (1836), *The Cause of the People of Malta; Now Before Parliament*, Effingham Wilson, London, 7-11.

Once said deadline lapses, said deputation shall be considered as approved and the deputies acknowledged as such, to whom can be truly trusted the interests of the Maltese Nation. Valletta 16 November 1801.'[16] The entire people ratified this procedure, as can be gleaned from the following two documents: 1. We the undersigned Magnificent Notaries[17] of the Grand Court of Valletta... Confirm that with regard to the notice mentioning the Deputies to be sent to London, that has been affixed in public places, nobody has appeared before us to protest or make other declarations, this 20 November 1801. Notary Emanuele Zarb; Notary Alessando Patrizio Spiteri. 2. I the undersigned Magnificent Notary of the Curiæ Capitanalis of Mdina confirm that the public notice regarding the deputation for London was affixed on 16 November 1801 in all the casals of Malta, inviting anybody who opposed such election, commission and departure to appear within three days in this court and bring forth said opposition, and that I was empowered to receive any such opposition until the lapse of said day, and that until today nobody has appeared to make any opposition. This 23 November 1801, Notary Calcedonio Bonello.–

This is the demonstration of the great doctrine of public law, namely: *The representatives and mandatories of the people cannot decide vital questions without the approval of their mandators,* that is to say without the consent of the people. Since the election and the mission of the deputation were accepted by the entire Nation, the deputies formulated a *Representation* addressed to His Majesty the King, *(a)* and the memorial on the National rights. *(b)* I add an excerpt from these in order to elucidate our Public law:

(a) Excerpt from the Representation:

'The Maltese were the first who took up arms against the French... The foreign troops were solely auxiliaries... During the blockade, the Maltese lost more than 20,000 souls. The British army had not a single soldier killed... The expenses of the war by land were defrayed by the Maltese; and, in order to enable them to do this, they mortgaged the lands of several villages. The Maltese therefore demand the possession of their Island by right of conquest from the French, who conquered it from the Order... As to the pretensions of this Order to the Island, it is our duty to assert, that it was ceded by the

---

16 Translated by the present author who could not find a contemporary translation.

17 *'Magnificent'* is the traditional title applied to a notary in Malta: *Manifk; Manifku Nutar*.

Emperor Charles the Fifth, in quality of fief... As to the landed property which that Order has acquired in Malta, it is contrary to the stipulations. The University,[18] the Monte di Pietà, and other institutions belong solely to the Maltese, are the property of individuals, and never did belong to the Order. Whatever pretensions the Knights of the Order of Saint John might have to the Island, they had forfeited them by an act much more conclusive than that of conquest, by the most unworthy treason to their own body, violating the sacred law of religion, honour, and the statutes of the Order... By this act, according to their own laws, they cease to be members of the Order, are degraded with infamy... But the Maltese have other pretentions to the sovereignty of their own Island. Without recurring to the maxim of some writers, that 'when the throne becomes vacant, the right of nominating the Sovereign devolves to the people,' the Maltese found their right to independence in having twice purchased Malta, and paid the stipulated price to the Kings of Spain and Sicily. King Alphonsus (to whose alto dominio, or suzerainty, our ancestors voluntarily submitted after having purchased the Island) in his diploma of the 27th of November 1397, declared that Malta formed a portion of his dominion; and in case any of his successors alienated it from the crown, under whatever title, whether as a government, or perpetual or temporary rectory, to any person whatever, even though he should be of the most exalted blood of the reigning Sovereign, Malta was to be preserved *'conjunctam semper tanquam membrumœ: Regie Corone, &c.;'* permitting the Maltese, in case of a contrary conduct, to resist 'manu forti pro quo in nullum crimen, delictum, vel in inobedientiam incurrere reputentur, et aliquatenus conseantur.' This was confirmed by King Ferdinando on the 4th of January 1489; the Maltese consider it as their Magna Charta, and confident they are, that a charter so dear to the English, will never be ravished from them, by that nation. With these privileges, Malta remained annexed to the crown of Sicily; and her inhabitants were treated by the King of Spain as a free people, until the reign of Charles the Fifth, who ceded the government to the Order of Saint John of Jerusalem... After a long negotiation, the Maltese submitted, but under the express condition, that they should enjoy their privileges for ever, and be considered as vassals, and annexed to the crown of Sicily; and that if the Order of Saint John should remove to another residence or establishment, Malta should return, as before, under the King of Sicily. They elected their Sovereigns, the Kings of Sicily, and governed their Island themselves. Placing a full reliance in the sincerity of the British government, and in the faith of the British nation, the Maltese were more desirous of becoming subjects of

[18] *Universitas.*

the King of England, and of enjoying all the advantages of free subjects of a Monarch who is the father of all his people, than to assert and maintain their own entire independence; but never did they suspect, nor can they now for a moment believe that, violating all the laws of justice, divine and human, they are to be forcibly delivered up by their auxiliary allies, as a conquered people, or as vile slaves, sold for a political consideration to other masters, to masters whose tyranny, extortion, and sacrilege, have rendered them the execration of every virtuous mind, and to whom, whatever horrible calamity may ensue, the Maltese nation while never submit... And it can be expected, that such a people will deliver up their privileges and their liberty to such masters? They may be free, they may perish in the attempt, but never will the Maltese submit![19]

'At whose hands will Divine Justice demand their blood? Upon whose head will the vengeance of Heaven fall; that vengeance which our fathers invoke, together with our innocent children, our venerable clergy, our wives, and our violated daughters?[20] Oh Britain, that so far has been the envy and the terror of tyrants, protector of freedom and of the oppressed! May your head that radiates glory never been struck by the thunder of the infallible hand of justice of he who gives and takes back crowns![21] His Britannic Majesty has never declared himself in any public act, or in any of the manifestations of his generals, our Sovereign. Never has he made use of any other title than that of Protector, however ardently the Maltese were desirous of being united with his subjects! We conceive it totally superfluous to enter into a detail of the indignities which the Maltese have received at the hands of the Order. What those men were, and what must have been the situation of their Government, may be conceived from this single fact – every one of them had betrayed his own order. To deliver up the Island of Malta to the Order would be the same as to deliver it over to the French.'[22]

(b) Excerpt from the memorial: 'The existence of the liberty of Malta to oppose the alienation and transfer to other powers was acknowledged by the same Order in the instructions given to two Ambassadors sent to Charles the Fifth on the 8th of October 1530, one of whom was a Knight of the Order

19 Translation borrowed from Cobbett's Annual Register, Vol. III, from January to June 1803, Cox and Baylis, London, July 1803, 674–677.

20 *Ibid.*, 677.

21 The present author's own translation, as Cobbett omits this part.

22 Corbett, 677.

and the other was a Maltese gentleman elected by the Council to represent to that Monarch that the Maltese had only adhered on condition that they should suffer no alteration of their privileges.

'When the Treaty of Amiens was officially communicated by the deputies of the Maltese Nation, the Popular Council made the following Declaration on the 15th of June 1802 on the rights of the inhabitants of the Islands of Malta and Gozo.

'We, the Members of the Congress of the Islands of Malta and Gozo, and their dependencies, by the free suffrage of the people, during the siege elected, to represent them on the important matter of ascertaining our native rights and privileges (enjoyed from time immemorial by our ancestors, for which, when encroached upon, we have shed our blood to regain them[23]), and of fixing a constitution of government, which shall secure to us, and our descendants in perpetuity, the happiness[24] of Freedom and the rights of just law, under the protection and Sovereignty of the King of a free people, His Majesty the King of the United Kingdom of Great Britain.[25] After along and mature deliberation, we make the following declaration, binding ourselves and our posterity for ever, on condition that our now acknowledged Prince[26] shall, on his part, fulfil and keep inviolate his compact with us.[27]

---

23 Here Bonello modifies the original text which refers to the ancestors having shed their blood.

24 Bonello uses *'felicità'* – I think this should be rendered as "happiness" rather than "blessings", bearing in mind the Enlightenment 'understanding of the first principles of law by which the natural world is governed, the idea that those first principles were discoverable by humans, and the belief that to pursue a life lived in accordance with those principles was to pursue a life of virtue, with the end result of happiness, best defined in the Greek sense of *eudaimonia* or human flourishing' – see C. N. Conklin (2015), 'The Origins of the Pursuit of Happiness', *Washington University Jurisprudence Review*, 7 Wash. U. Jur. Rev. 195 (2015), 195–262, *passim.*

25 Bonello omits *'and Ireland'*.

26 Bonello omits 'and Sovereign'.

27 Translation borrowed in its entirety from *The Appeals of the Nobility and People of Malta, to the Justice, Public Faith, and Policy, of the British Government, for the Fulfilment of the conditions upon which they gave up their Island to the King, namely, their Ancient Rights, under a Free Constitution,* Henry Reynell, London, 1811, 52 *et seq.*

'1st. That the King of the United Kingdom of Great Britain[28] is our Sovereign Lord, and his lawful successors shall, in all times to come, be acknowledged as our lawful Sovereigns.

'2nd. That His said Majesty has no right to cede these Islands to any power. That, if he chooses to withdraw his protection, and abandon his sovereignty, the right of electing another Sovereign, or of governing these Islands, belongs to us, the inhabitants[29] alone, and without control.

'3rd. That His Majesty's governors or representatives of these Islands and their dependencies are, and shall ever be, bound to observe and keep inviolate[30] the constitution, which with the sanction[31] of said Britannic[32] Royal Majesty, or his representative or plenipotentiary, shall be established for[33] us, composing the General Congress elected by the people, in the following proportion, viz:

'The Cities: Notabile and Casal Dingli 14 members, Valletta 12, Vittoriosa 4, Senglea 4, Cospicua 4.

'The Casals:[34] Birchircara 5, Attard 2, Lia and Balzan 3, Curmi 12, Naxaro 4, Gargur 3, Musta 5, Zebbug 8, Siggieui 4, Luca 3, Gudia 1, Zurigo 4, Micabiba 2, Crendi 2, Zabbar 3, Tarxen 2, Asciach 1.

'Total 104 members.

'4th. That the people of Malta, Gozo, and their representatives in Popular Council assembled, have a right to send letters, or deputies, to the foot of the throne, to represent and to complain of violation of rights and privileges, or of acts contrary to the constitution of the government, or of the spirit thereof.

'5th. That the right of legislation and taxation belongs to the Consiglio

---

28 Bonello again omits *'and Ireland'*.

29 Bonello omits *'and aborigines'*.

30 *Appeals* uses *'inviolable'*.

31 Bonello omits *'and ratification'*.

32 *Appeals* uses *'British'*.

33 Bonello uses *'per'*, *'for'*; *Appeals 'by'*, *'da'*.

34 Bonello omits *'or Burghs'*.

Popolare, with the consent and assent of His Majesty's representatives.[35]

'6th. That His Majesty, the King, is the protector of our holy religion, and is bound to uphold and protect it as heretofore;[36] and that His Majesty's representatives have a right to claim such church honours, as have always been shown to the regents of these islands.

'7th. The interference, in matters spiritual or temporal, of no other temporal Sovereign shall be admitted in these islands; and reference, in spiritual matters, shall only be had to the Pope, and to the respective generals of the monastic orders.

'8th. That freemen have a right to choose their own religion. Toleration of other religions is therefore established, as a right; but no sect is permitted to molest, insult, or disturb those of other religious professions.

'9th. That no man whatsoever has any personal authority over the lives, property, or liberty of another. Power resides only in the law;[37] and restraint, or punishment, can only be exercised in obedience to law.'[38]

On that same day, the representatives sent to Governor Ball an address in which they declared that 'since the remotest times, much before the arrival of the Order in Malta, the Maltese could convoke a Popular Council. This Council kept functioning fully even under the reign of the Order, but over time its strength was weakened and in the year 1775 it was completely extinguished. This caused the rights of the Maltese to be scorned with impunity. From then onward, the full force of despotism felt, and the Maltese could not impede the fatalities that happened, and the misfortunes suffered. For these reasons, the Maltese want to restore it... The utility of the exercise of this right for the Maltese would be huge as demonstrated by those times in which it functioned... The Maltese thus pray to be free to make use of this right, not because they do not have the full faculty of doing so, but because in these circumstances they consider necessary this Government's participation

---

35 Bonello omits *'without which the people are not bound'*.

36 Bonello omits *'and without any diminution of what has been practised since these islands have acknowledged His Majesty as their Sovereign to this days'*.

37 Bonello omits the emphasis (expressed through italicisation) found in the *Appeals* version.

38 Bonello again omits the emphasis (expressed through italicisation) found in the *Appeals* version.

by granting immediate approval if it is so ordered by the Court. Upon the Order's return to Malta, the same right would already be in place allowing the Maltese to enjoy the advantages and, should the Order not return, the Maltese would receive their real rights. For if the Order does not return to Malta, as it currently seems to be the case, and there would be the need to make new arrangements for the future state of these islands, we pray you in the name of our Nation, justice, humanity, and all divine and human laws, to use all your credit for the consideration of the rights of the Maltese by which they have been authorised by their former Sovereigns to give their consent to any change in their Government. This consent cannot be neglected without violating justice; and this we do not expect from a just Government.'[39]

The Treaty of Amiens not having come into effect, and for this reason, neither the rules established by it with regard to Malta, Lord Melville declared in Parliament[40] on 24 May 1803:[41] 'That the British Government and the inhabitants of Malta establish between themselves the form of Government of the Island; and that they be protected by a British garrison...'.[42]

But since this was not carried out, in 1811 a Petition was sent to His Majesty the King in Council, in which the Maltese demanded the restitution of their ancient sacred rights, violated by the latter Grand Masters of the Order of St. John—enjoyed by us during the siege of Valletta—expressly stipulated when, with unlimited confidence, we delivered up our islands to the King's officers—afterwards taken from us — and again solemnly promised us in the name of the King, by his representative, Sir Charles Cameron. Thus, the Maltese demanded the following: 1st. A free representation of the people, or Popular Council. 2nd. Independent tribunals. 3rd. A free press. 4th. Trial by Jury, as in England, and according to the ancient usage, the right of appeal from the sentence of the Judges of the Popular Council.[43] 5th. A constitution which

---

39 The full version of this letter, without Bonello's omissions, can be found in Azopardi, *op. cit.*, 253–255.

40 House of Lords.

41 It seems that Lord Melville spoke on 23 *not 24* May – see Corbett, under Parliamentary Debates, 1662–1663 *et seq*.

42 I have been unable to find these words. What I have found instead is this: '... *the people of Malta, under a form of government agreeable to their wishes, were now established under the protection of Great Britain*' (Corbett, 1663).

43 In Mitrovich, *op. cit.*, 19, one finds: 'either in the manner practised in England, or according to our own ancient usage, which was an appeal in every case from the sentence of the Judges to the *Consiglio Popolare*'.

shall unite the spirit of our ancient, free, and only legitimate government, with that of the English constitution.[44] The petitioners' parting shot: 'For the purpose of securing our ancient rights, we elected for our Sovereign His Majesty the King of Great Britain. In the name of justice, of humanity, of all laws, human and divine, and by the lives of twenty thousand persons lost during the siege of Valletta, we beg you to employ all your credit and energy to have the rights and privileges of the Maltese taken into consideration. According to these rights, our ancient Sovereigns could not impose on us any form of government without our own consent—a consent which cannot be dispensed with without the violation of justice, and which violation we are far from expecting from a government so cordially elected by us.'[45] The local Government declared the petition as an act of partisanship, etc, but still had to send it to the Metropolitan Government and then propose the measures required in the circumstances. These Commissioners received memorials from various distinguished persons, of which I shall transcribe the following excerpts:

> Monsignor F. Onorato Bres, Maltese, wrote to the Royal Commissioners on 8 July 1812: 'The illustrious late Lord Melville proposed that the British Government and the inhabitants of Malta should establish between them the Government of the island... Undoubtedly, gentlemen, the enlightened will accept to consult with the inhabitants – those, that is, who are honestly attached to their homeland, to Great Britain, and not the wicked egotists who, by sacrificing their country, seek to enrich themselves... Since nothing can be agreed upon unless there is agreement on the principles, the first writing that I have the merit of addressing to you deals with the principles that have to be adopted when establishing the constitution and laws of Malta, and it goes without saying that these should be *liberal principles*, and not *restricted* and advised by miserable politics. Putting aside the general arguments, there is no need to highlight that men always try to conserve the enjoyment of their existence, honour and wealth, and to make sure of this they try to sacrifice as little as possible their natural freedom in favour of civil

44 Translation borrowed from Mitrovich, 18-19.

45 *Ibid.*

society. An equitable, just and free Government seeks to acquire in every way the goodwill and the loyalty of the governed. The despotism and arbitrariness of he who has authority produce discontent among the subjects, who seek every opportunity to free themselves of the oppression and such opportunity, sooner or later, presents itself. These truths are certainly not unknown to personalities hailing from a country where a constitution reigns that, despite the shortcomings that one expects it might have, is the freest and the best that currently exist in Europe – it follows that I do not need to digress on this. Then again, I am convinced that you are endowed with such healthy morality that you do not consider just elsewhere that which in your country you deem iniquitous. Undoubtedly, in England you look at arbitrariness and oppression with the greatest horror, and consider them as a moral plague... Thus, when you propose the laws for the Maltese, I am convinced that you will adapt the principles of freedom; to encourage you in this praiseworthy determination, I will propose three very valid reasons. In establishing the form of Government of Malta, you should follow the principles of freedom, 1st. Because Malta always had a free Government; 2nd. Because you cannot in any way consider Malta as a conquered country; 3rd. Because it is mostly in England's interest that this island have a fair Government, and free.' Having the Monsignor made these three points: Moreover, the Maltese have to have their votes heeded because England has granted her colonies a form of Government similar to her own, that is to say a free Government...

'Is Malta less important for Great Britain than Jamaica? Why should Malta be denied what was granted to Jamaica? As a matter of fact, Malta has the right to demand to be treated better than Jamaica, because she was not conquered and she enjoyed a free Government in the past. From what I have said you can clearly gather that Malta can never be regarded as a country conquered by England, and that justice does not allow the imposition of a servile yoke on the forelimbs of the Maltese. You have to see that all the wrongs they have suffered be righted, giving them back the freedom which they regained with much sacrifice... The Maltese request a free Government and ask for nothing other than the conservation of their ancient privileges which endowed them with this benefit. It has never been praiseworthy to take away privileges from subjects, and it was always a dangerous and unattractive principle, because men are very much attached to their privileges which they consider as their fundamental law, constitution and Magna Charta. When they see that they have been deprived of these privileges, they abhor the Government, and often seek how to shake it. We clearly remember how when Joseph II took away their privileges from the Flemish, the House of Austria lost the low countries. And for the same reason, it did not receive from Hungary in the last wars the same help that in the days of Maria Theresa saved the Austrian Monarchy. I tell you this because I assure you on my honour that I am very attached to Great Britain and I am very much committed that England should forever conserve Malta, being Malta so useful to her, and therefore wish to avoid the great grief of my fellow citizens in seeing that the Sicilians, thanks to the English, enjoy a free constitution and free laws, whereas my fellow citizens are deprived of such good... Do they not desire to return under the dominion of His Majesty the King of the Two Sicilies, as was the case prior to 1530? What honour does this bring to England? Gentlemen, remember that you belong to a generous Nation. Therefore you have to reflect before you propose the form of Government that suits Malta, whether it is more expedient to adopt liberal principles, not only for the happiness of a people, but also to conserve for the British Empire this highly important parade ground.[46] Or to follow opposite principles with the very probable danger of losing, sooner or later, the possession of Malta. If you, Gentlemen, are, as I am convinced, endowed with a modicum of good sense, you cannot hesitate even for a moment on this latter alternative; and I would have won the case I'm pleading.'

46 '*Piazza*', clearly a synecdoche.

The same Prelate, in another letter dated 24 August 1812, wrote to the same Commissioners:

> 'It is the honour, or rather the duty, of everyone to seek the good of the society in which they live – said Mr Laing, the Public Secretary at the orders of His Excellency the Royal Civil Commissioner in the Notification printed last 24 July... Whoever thinks deeply on civil society recognises that there can be no better guarantor of the good of any State than the Council of the representatives of the Nation freely chosen by the same... Had the Maltese never enjoyed the privilege of having the Popular Council then undoubtedly the Most Clement Sovereign would grant it. How could it be otherwise? A Prince who does not have the insane and iniquitous desire to oppress, to tyrannise over his subjects, knowing that he was constituted by the Most High God to seek their happiness, how can he ever obtain their happiness if he does not establish the way to bring to the throne common representations? How can this be done without a Popular Council? ... Our August Sovereign should grant the Maltese this Council; because he is not an Asiatic or African Sovereign, accustomed despotically to rule his subjects, but the King of a free people that always upheld principles liberal and never oppressive. Thus, it is natural for him to want the good of his subjects in whichever part of the world they might be. It was for this very reason that the Maltese chose him for their Sovereign. But how can he ever learn whether his beloved subjects of Malta are oppressed or happy, without the Popular Council? Any private supplication would either not reach the throne or else it would be given an unfavourable interpretation, branding it as the product of partisanship... The Maltese have the right to expect this benefit from His Majesty as effect of His Royal protection of which a foremost Minister of His Majesty said: The attachment, loyalty, and good conduct of the people of Malta and Gozo had entitled them to whatever protection it was in His Majesty's power to grant. So far I have spoken about the hypothesis that Malta never had

> the privilege of this Council. What will be said if it can be proven that she did enjoy such privilege? Would it not be a great injustice if Malta were currently to be denied this privilege should its past exercise be proven after His Majesty's Representatives repeatedly solemnly promised to the Maltese the enjoyment of their privileges?...'

The Monsignor then shows how the First Lord of the Treasury, Count Liverpool, during the negotiations on the Peace of Amiens, declared that the Popular Council could be restored, having already existed on this Island; and continues, 'Undoubtedly, His Excellency the Count Liverpool cannot have in 1803 proposed to restore in Malta the National Council as beneficial to the Maltese and in 1812 deem that the Maltese should not have this privilege again. His eminent virtues, his inward greatness, and the sublime nature of his ideas keep him from changing his mind because in 1803 he believed that the Order should regain Malta while in 1812 at the Court of St James's it was resolved to conserve her forever united to Great Britain'.

The Prelate then shows that His Majesty had recognised the legality of the Popular Council, since the Envoys nominated by the Popular Council to remonstrate against the *restoration* of the Order in Malta submitted a memorial to His Majesty that was then sent to Amiens, communicated to Bonaparte, and mentioned in the protocol of the Peace Congress of Amiens (*Pièces officielles aux préliminaries et au traité d'Amiens*, p. 166) and later, Lord Hobart, Minister at the orders of His Majesty, sent to the Popular Council's deputies an official copy of the Peace Treaty of Amiens.

The Marquis Testaferrata and other distinguished citizens insisted with the Commissioners that the Popular Council be once again established, and on the other freedoms of the country.

The dates referred to serve as evidence that Malta always had, not only in virtue of the natural law but also of positive terms, self-government. Neither was she conquered, but united to the Kingdom of the Two Sicilies as a free people, accepted the Order according to conditions and (once the French had been evicted) spontaneously united with Great Britain as was expressly acknowledged by the Malta Government Gazette of 27 June 1814 that, publishing the principal articles of the Treaty of Paris of the 30 and 31 May of that same year with regard to Malta, said: 'The island of Malta and its dependencies shall belong in full right and sovereignty to his Britannic majesty. – The Maltese may well congratulate themselves upon the fact that, in virtue of this treaty, Malta and its Dependencies belong from this date to Great Britain, she being then in possession of the Islands, due to the voluntary donation made her of them by the Maltese in 1802.'[47] This spontaneous union was also mentioned in the House of Commons on 7 June 1836 by Mr A.W. Beauclerk: 'It should be recollected that we did not acquire that Island by our own troops. The brave Maltese gave themselves up to our protection, on conditions, which had been broken through.'[48]

(These words were reported by the *Gazzetta di Malta* on 13 June 1836, No. 1333).

It is worth summarising the rights which the people exercised in virtue of said self-government:

(a) It had its Council, the members of which, as we have seen, at the time of the blockade, were elected by all the heads of family, that is by suffrage almost universal. The representatives exercised *legislative power*, managing all the affairs of the island. (b) The *Universitates* were *Municipalities*. (c) *Judicial power* was in the hands of the natives; the citizens could not be summoned before foreign judges, not even before the Sicilians during the union with the Kingdom of the Two Sicilies; the Judges were elected; all this can be gathered from the Representation of the Jurats of Mdina and of Valletta, of February 1809, presented to the Commissioner, of which I transcribe the more important points: – *The Magistrates of Mdina and of Valletta present to Your Excellency the reasons and rights with which the Maltese Nation is endowed to oppose any attempt that threatens to transfer cognisance of a certain type of legal action concerning Commerce to the Vice-Admiralty court or any other court composed of foreigners. – When the Royal House of Aragon acquired sovereignty, the Maltese obtained the privilege of being exempt from summons outside their homeland in their cases at first instance. – In 1455, the Maltese obtained that the citizens would elect an Appeals Judge, and since his jurisdiction was limited, it was extended in 1458 to all types of cases. In 1429, it was established that all ministers who exercise administrative and judicial authority*

47 Translation borrowed from William Hardman (1909), *A History of Malta during the Period of the French and British Occupations 1798–1815* Part II, Longmans, London, 647.

48 Translation borrowed from Anon. (1846), *Important Notices of Malta and Gozo*, Anglo-Maltese Printing Press, Malta, 13.

always be Maltese, in 1438 that they be elected by the citizens, in 1466 that they be nationals who reside on these Islands, in 1458 and 1475 that the Governor,[49] *the then-Prime Minister of the Island, hail from the principal citizens, and that the way elections of officials was done be invariable. These privileges conserved their force under the Government of the Order. Since it was inevitable to take to the Council of the Order the legal actions of the members of the Hierosolymitan Order and of the Treasury, all the Judges of the Maltese courts would join the members of said Council on all occasions to judge the cases in which Maltese parties were involved, whether as plaintiffs or accused, and having a casting vote like the Lords of the Council. – The Maltese Nation is convinced that His Majesty is determined to increase rather than decrease their Nation's privileges as repeatedly affirmed in the proclamations of the Royal Commissioner Cameron and of General Pigot published on 15 February and 23 July 1801 and in the letter of General Pigot of 14 February 1801.* (d) With regard to the *Executive Power,* King Alfonso undertook in 1438 that the officials and office-holders of Malta and Gozo would be freely elected by the citizens. A rescript of 17 January 1466 laid down that the same person could not occupy more than one office. The Jurats and the Governor were bound to obey all the resolutions of the Popular Council... King Alfonso permitted with his reply to the letter sent by the *Universitas* on 6 June 1441, to not obey illegitimate ordinances. – The people partook of the executive power even through various committees, that administered different branches of the public service... As to *communal affairs,* there were in each casal since ancient times, *Connestabili* who oversaw public order, quelled quarrels, helped the criminal official, represented the people before the Governor and the Jurats. They were first nominated by the Jurats and then elected by the people. (e) *Public finances* were under the direction and the control of the representatives of the people. (f) The Council exercised the right and duty to *provide for public needs*; as I have outlined above in many examples. (g) The representatives, as we have seen, sent Envoys even to Sovereigns, and received the Envoy of the Russian Emperor, the Chevalier Italisky, with whom they exchanged diplomatic correspondence; on occasion they therefore administered *foreign affairs.* (h) The Popular Council had the right of *superior surveillance.* – Furthermore, the Jurats of Mdina reviewed the works of the Governor and his judge as well as the work of the Jurats who left office; as transpires from the following document:

---

49 *Capitano della Verga,* the *Ħakem.*

‘I, Stefano Sillato, usher of the office of the Jurats, declare that I have published banns on 2 September 1573 that whoever intends to move complaints or accusations against the Jurats, the Governor, and the Judge who were in office during the past year, has to appear before the Three Jurats now sitting on the Court bench.’

These rights naturally nourished the sentiment for freedom, that has always been dear to the Maltese, as they abundantly proved on all occasions. I cannot, unless I overstep the limits of this short work, enumerate all the cases in which my forefathers stood up as a single man to defend their liberties that had been passed from one generation to the next. Suffice it to mention but two: 1st. The resistance mounted when the Order tried to dismantle Mdina – to abolish the ancient *Universitas*; the resistance was so widespread that even the women took part in it, and the Order was forced to abandon the enterprise; 2nd. The confrontation with the French for which General Ball addressed these words to the Maltese: *‘That circumstance gave me the opportunity to witness your bravery and the public virtues you deployed in defending the sacred cause of liberty. The pen of history will describe on its eternal tables better than I the illustrious example of heroism that you showed before a stunned Europe.’*[50] (Ball’s address when he was presented a sword of honour.)

As we have seen, the Maltese always requested their rights. When their legitimate requests expressed in 1811 were not granted, in 1836 they presented, through Mr Ewart of the House of Commons, a popular petition asking for freedom of the press, a municipal body, a popular council analogous to the one that had existed, etc... We all know the great commitment in the promotion of this petition shown by the Baron Camillo Sceberras, gloriously remembered, Mr Giorgio Mitrovich, and other meritorious and distinguished citizens; as well as the results of that step and the reforms introduced in 1849.

It is therefore not necessary to argue at length that those reforms were insufficient. For this reason, in 1864, the population made a new popular petition with which it requested self-government, requesting a Council that was truly efficient, to which would be entrusted (in addition to ordinary law-making functions) the treasury and public property... In reply to this petition, the Metropolitan Government ordered that great consideration should be

50 Translated by the present author.

shown to the opinions of the Elected Members of Council in matters of local and domestic interest, and that above all, no vote of money should be pressed against the majority of the Elected members,[51] that with regard to consolidated expenses, a draft local bill be submitted for the approval of the Crown, and that necessary information be supplied on the way to establish municipal institutions. But it also declared that the requested reform of the Council was not necessary, since it gave enough space for the representatives of the people to exercise all the control that was convenient on the public administration.

In this reply, nothing is clearly explained. Except the opinion of the Minister for the Colonies[52] that there is no real necessity to reform the current Council. – This reply rejects the fundamental point, and equivocates with regard to all the other points. But this negation, and this equivocation, serve only to make more evident the need for radical reform and our right to obtain it: just like the shadow makes the light stand out. Clearly, all the efforts of the reactionaries have been fruitless. The reaction serves only to invigorate those against whom it is directed. Public opinion may be scorned, oppressed, targeted and insulted, but it will all rebound and damage whoever despises it. At times, the people observes temporary silence, giving the impression that it will no longer be anxious, and yet it moves.

The people today is quiet. But it will raise its voice again before the House of Commons of Great Britain. The people will say: This land is mine; my forefathers bought it, when it was given as collateral by the Kings of the past, with their money. I redeemed it when it was oppressed by the French; these institutes of public charity are pious foundations of our dear ancestors; public money is the product of our sweat and blood and no part of it can be taken away from our disposition, our control, as this is not admitted by the sacred law of property that embraces the faculty to dispose both of belongings as well as of their fruits, and it is not admitted by the constitution and the popular sentiment of England. The entire administration concerns our affairs, and the disposition of the affairs of others without those others' consent is a

51 Though Bonello does not quote directly, he is here reporting in Italian the following text originally written in English from *'great consideration'* to *'of the Elected members'* – from the letter of Secretary of State for the Colonies Edward Cardwell to Governor John Gaspard Le Marchant, 19 September 1864. See Hilda I. Lee (1972), *Malta 1813–1914: A Study in Constitutional and Strategic Development*, Progress Press, Malta, 140.

52 Secretary of State for the Colonies.

violation of the law. The people will say: Our requests do not overstep our rights that we have possessed since time immemorial. Our requests do not offend in any way the interests of the British Empire. On the contrary, they augment the moral form of its people, for whom the highest prestige is that of being the standard-bearers of freedom. Freedom does not suffer oppression; thus, England freed with great sacrifice the slaves in her Colonies, and the immortal Abraham Lincoln followed suit in the United States. The people will say: We have not been conquered, we united ourselves with the British Monarchy out of our free will, and it promised to maintain our sacred rights. Can the Great English Nation forget the word it gave?

One people understands another people... The representatives of Great Britain will listen to our legitimate reclamations, and our plebiscite will be heeded and carried out with the help of the very same Metropolitan Government that now considers it inopportune. *La lumière va son train, et le soleil achève sa course* (Bossuet).

Yes, our longed-for rights will triumph. But we must be united, steadfast and perseverant in our requests. This is our sacred duty, so much for the present so as not to be considered pusillanimous and forgetful of our duty, as much as for the future so that posterity will not accuse us of ignominy, of having been degenerate sons of the ancient Maltese, unable to regain in this century of light[53] that National Freedom that our beloved forefathers succeeded in establishing in the murkiness of the dark Middle Ages. – If, by any chance, there is anybody who believes himself not bound to employ his energy for this purpose, because the country is small and the population not big, I tell him that it has often happened that small peoples pushed for civilisation more than the big ones, and that the law, which is the basis of our progress and prosperity, is so common to all of humankind that if the freedom of a people, no matter how small, or even of a single individual, is harmed, then the rights of the all of humanity suffer.

It thus follows that the defence of the law is the main concern of everybody who feels human dignity... I therefore felt bound to add with this somehow defective publication to the elucidation of our freedoms. I will deem myself fortunate if I have managed to push forward the sentiment of Common Liberty, and if I have managed in my intent to outline our Public Law as limpidly as the task requires. I will be satisfied if this my little work

53 [‘*Secolo di luce*’.]

motivates those who have more preparation and energy for the cogitation of this subject on which no treatise has yet appeared (!), I will be fully satisfied if I would have sufficiently fulfilled the role of whetstone, which serves to sharpen, but itself does not cut.

Who was Amabile Bonello?

Born on 31 November 1836 in Valletta, son of Ferdinando Bonello and Concetta *née* Mattei, Amabile was sent at the age of five to live with a relative in Tripoli, Libya, to learn the rudiments of business. He returned to Malta in 1848, and studied Italian, English, and "business studies".[54] At 19 years old, he was employed as a clerk with a company, but continued studying part-time with the Hungarian "Fulvery Agos"[55] who not only knew Latin but had also written 'numerous works of public law'.[56] Bonello was also the editor of *L'Emigrazione Maltese* (1867–1877), a paper aimed at encouraging Maltese emigration to North Africa.[57]

He died on 19 January 1878, having drowned off the coast of Tas-Sliema after having spent the evening dining with friends.[58]

The political context in 1867 Malta

In 1849, Malta was granted a new Constitution that had two main characteristics: (i) decision-making powers were retained by the Crown Colony Government, while (ii) an elective principle was introduced.[59] The

---

54 *Cenni Biografici in Memoria dell'Amico e Patriota Amabile Bonello,* Tipografia del *Risorgimento,* Malta, 1879, 3-4.

55 According to my Hungarian sources, neither is "Fulvery" a Hungarian name nor "Agos" a Hungarian surname. Possibly the surname was "Akos".

56 *Cenni Biografici,* 4. The present author has managed to find no such work penned by "Fulvery Agos".

57 Arnold Cassola (2000), *The Literature of Malta: An Example of Unity in Diversity,* Minima Publishing, Malta, 198. Bonello's ideas on emigration were supported by Mikiel Anton Vassalli's son M.A. Vassalli Formose de Fremaux – M.A. Vassalli Formose de Fremaux (1867), *Suggestions in Accordance With Mr. Amabile Bonello's Project of Emigration in the Coasts of North Africa,* Malta, *passim.*

58 *Cenni Biografici,* 7–8. I am not being frugal with the details – these are the only biographical highlights supplied by his closest friends, the paucity of which necessarily raises more questions than it answers.

59 J.J. Cremona (1997), *The Maltese Constitution and Constitutional History*

Maltese were dissatisfied as, to borrow Hilda Lee's words, they considered that '[t]he Governor retained all the absolutism that had been possessed prior to 1849, only [...] that his actions were cloaked under the semblance of a representative institution'.[60]

In January 1864, a petition was sent to the Secretary of State for the Colonies demanding constitutional reform (more control and decision-making powers with regard to local matters) and the appointment of a Civil Governor.[61] Among the reactions received by the Metropolitan Government was Governor Le Marchant's: '[t]hese islands from many circumstances are necessarily precluded from a form of constitution embodying a Representative Legislature, or what is commonly called "responsible government" and are unsuited to it'.[62]

In December 1865, newly-appointed Governor Storks was sent by the Colonial Office to Jamaica to investigate the manner in which the rebellion there had been quelled. On his return, Storks established District Committees in Malta and Gozo, that were to be elected by the people but would have only a consultative function and no power to spend public money. Secretary of State Cardwell doubted 'whether the Maltese population [were] ripe for any executive powers'.[63]

Before the expiration of his term, Storks increased the salary of an official, raising the ire of the Maltese elected Council members, five of whom resigned in protest, though the resignations 'produced only slight

---

Since 1813 (2nd ed.), PEG, Malta, 13-14.

60 Lee, 136.

61 *Ibid.*, 137.

62 *Ibid.*, 138. It seems that Le Marchant held these ideas in general. For instance, while occupying the post of Governor of Newfoundland, Le Marchant strongly opposed the colony's request made in 1851 for responsible government. He asserted that the Newfoundland *'still lacked the social structure, the political cohesiveness and a large enough assembly (then possessing only fifteen members) in which parties or political groups, not sectarian rivals, would compete for power, control the civil service, govern in the interests of the whole community, and retire from office (without ruin to themselves) when defeated'* – John Manning Ward (1976), *Colonial Self-Government: The British Experience 1759-1856*, Macmillan, London, 314.

63 Lee, 141-142.

excitement'.[64] Though the new Governor, General Patrick Grant, 'concluded that this was a practical proof of the indifference of the Maltese on the issue',[65] the press kept campaigning for a Civil Governor and for a new petition to the House of Commons.

This was the historical moment in which Bonello wrote his essay.

The Maltese Petition was eventually presented, promoting, to quote Lee again,

> the claims made earlier in the 1830s for the establishment of a Congresso Popolare. [...] They requested the appointment of a Civil Governor, and a reform of the constitution to enable the elected members to exercise a preponderance in questions concerning public expenditure, public property and all other matters of local and domestic policy.[66]

Bonello's thesis

Bonello's essay is clearly meant to keep the morale high. The implicit main thrust of the argument seems to be that, even though the 1800 capitulation articles made no mention of a representative Council, the ancient constitution of Malta – that had been constantly observed by successive sovereigns, even though it had been trampled upon by the last Grand Masters – had envisaged such a Council. Bonello tries vividly to outline the unwritten, autochthonous constitution of Malta, based on the representation of the will of the Nation, a constitution that for centuries had permitted self-government to the Maltese.

It is beyond the compass of the present study to discuss the self-governing polities of Christendom, that is Medieval Europe. Of more direct pertinence would be the following excerpt from an anonymous 1817 publication pointing at an English scenario similar to Bonello's Medieval Malta:

> Long before the revolution settlement, it was the constitution of England, that laws should be made not merely by act of parliament; for in that case any assembly

64 *Ibid.*, 142.

65 *Ibid.*

66 *Ibid.*

> convened by the king and called a parliament, might have made laws binding on the people: but they were to be made with the common consent of the whole commonalty of the land by act of parliament; and then they had the only constitutional sanction of any law, not tacitly adopted and acquiesced in by the people themselves, and by general use and approbation become an indisputable custom. Bearing this in mind, we may better understand the celebrated declaration of the rights and liberties of the subject, which has often been called the foundation and main support our constitution, although, in fact, it was but an imperfect recital of previously established laws, which had in former times been more explicitly and unequivocally declared.[67]

Was Bonello implicitly but wittingly referring to this English political history/"mythology"? Or was there a common Europe-wide past and Bonello was merely referring to the Maltese past (whether fact or mythology[68]) sincerely believing that the Maltese case had been unique? It is difficult to say from the essay. What we can say for sure is that 'the appeal to consent is orthodox common law doctrine, which can be traced back as far as Glanvill and Bracton, and even behind that to the Justinianic code'.[69] In other words, the Maltese were presenting an argument that had to resonate with their English interlocutors, and, in my estimation, it did. But the Colonial Office was more preoccupied with strategic and military matters than legal

---

67 Anon. (1817), *Common consent, the basis of the Constitution of England; or, Parliamentary Reform considered and tried by the tests of Law and Reason*, Thomas and Joseph Allman, London, 23. Interestingly, the frontispiece of this book carries a quotation *in Italian* from Fra. Paolo (Sarpi).

68 Victor Mallia-Milanes (1988) in 'The Genesis of Maltese Nationalism' in Victor Mallia-Milanes (ed.), *The British Colonial Experience 1800-1964: The Impact on Maltese Society*, Mireva, Malta, 13, explains: 'To the public mind, these "rights" were believed to have been traditionally invested in such national institutions as the *Consiglio Popolare* and the *Università*. The basis of this "belief" may, indeed, be partly or wholly mythical; nonetheless, in terms of pure popular psychology, what matters is not whether such beliefs correspond to historical truth [...] but whether they are genuinely embedded in emotional reality'.

69 Gerard J. Postema (2003), 'Classical Common Law Jurisprudence (Part II)', *Oxford University Commonwealth Law Journal*, Summer 2003, 1–28, p 22–23.

history and theory. Indeed, following the 1869 petition, the new Secretary of State wrote, 'I presume the theory respecting the Government of Malta is this – that in its peculiar circumstances the Crown must have extensive powers, for the safety of the place, and of its garrison – but that in local matter that do not [impair] Imperial interests the greatest attention should be paid to the wishes of the representatives of the Maltese population'.[70]

Romagnosi

The quotation opening Bonello's essay is from Gian Domenico Romagnosi's[71] *Introduzione allo Studio del Diritto Pubblico Universale,*[72] and it is doctored. Before analysing it, a few lines on Romagnosi's philosophical thought.

Romagnosi's "universal public law" is wider than our contemporary notion of "Public law": it includes the civil law as well as links to politics and morals; it is a mixture of *positive* public law and *natural* law. He seeks to demonstrate that the ultimate end of collective human life is "happiness", achieved only through the multilateral perfection of society.[73] Derived from neither Montesquieu nor Britain (which he considered too aristocratic), and not even from Napoleon, Romagnosi's model – government to represent the land-owners, educated citizens, and members of the military – contemplated a series of constitutional organs, such as a Legislative Council, a Senate, and a Protectorate (a constitutional arbiter). For Romagnosi, the Sovereign is higher 'in law and in fact' to each citizen but not to 'the united body of the nation', in which lies 'the ultimate constitutional guarantee'.[74]

The quotation[75] is a doctored version of the response to question §261.

---

70 Lee, 143.

71 (1761–1835)

72 "Introduction to the Study of Universal Public Law" (1805).

73 Carla de Pascale (2012), 'Romagnosi, Gian Domenico' in A. Clericuzio, S. Ricci (eds.), *Il contributo italiano alla storia del Pensiero – Filosofia*, Istituto della Enciclopedia Italiano, (online edition).

74 Gian Paolo Romagnani (2017), 'Romagnosi, Giovanni Domenico' in *Dizionario Biografico degli Italiani* Vol. 88, Treccani, Rome.

75 Gian Domenico Romagnosi (1814), *Introduzione alla Studio del Diritto Pubblico Universale* in *Scritti sul Diritto Filosofico di G.D. Romagnosi, riordinati ed illustrati da Alessandro de Giorgi*, Frascona-Barbera, Palermo, 101.

Romagnosi's original

Allorché pertanto avviene il caso, in cui giustamente il privato vantaggio attuale possa venire sacrificato al pubblico, egli rassomiglia a quello di un buon padre di famiglia, il quale con economia fa macinare il suo grano, e toglie alcuna cosa del pane che dà alla propria famiglia per salvare la semente dell'anno venturo, affinchè non provi gli orrori della fame. In breve = egli è un sacrifizio d'un reale ma minor bisogno degl'individui particolari, che per necessità vien fatto ad un loro maggior bisogno.

When there is thus a case in which it is fair that a present private benefit can be sacrificed in favour of a public benefit, this recalls the case of the good family man, who frugally has his grain ground and removes something from the bread that he gives to his family in order to save the seeds for the coming year, to avoid that they go through the horrors of hunger. In brief = it is the sacrifice of a real but smaller need of particular individuals, which out of necessity is done for their greater need.

Bonello's version

Allorché **‖** *avviene il grave caso, in cui* **‖** *positivamente il privato vantaggio* **‖** *deve o possa venire sagrificato al pubblico,* **‖** *in allora è uopo ricordare il buon padre di famiglia, il quale con economia fa macinare il suo grano, e toglie alcuna cosa del pane, che dà alla propria famiglia per salvare la semente dell'anno venturo, affinchè non provi gli orrori della fame.* **‖** *Purtroppo egli è un sacrifizio d'un reale ma minore bisogno degl'individui particolari, che per necessità vien fatto ad un loro* **‖** *migliore bisogno.*

When there is **‖** a serious case in which *positively* a **‖** private benefit must or can be sacrificed in favour of a public benefit, **‖** then it is necessary to recall the good family man, who frugally has his grain ground and removes something from the bread that he gives to his family, in order to save the seeds for the coming year, to avoid that they go through the horrors of hunger. **‖** Unfortunately, it is the sacrifice of a real but *smaller* need of particular individuals, which out of necessity is done for their **‖** *better* need.

Romagnosi explains that, 'according to nature, never – except when fairness so necessitates – should the private good be really sacrificed for the public good'.[76] By "fairness", he means that for the individual to be expected to sacrifice his private interest for the public, the public interest should also be a private interest, but understood as deriving from public (as opposed to) private relations.[77]

Bonello shifts Romagnosi's cautious reasoning, from choice ('can') to obligation ('must', 'necessary', 'unfortunately'). He further shifts Romagnosi's quantitative comparison ('smaller'→'greater') to a qualitative one ('smaller'→'better'). As Bonello's motivation is clearly rhetorical, its analysis lies beyond the scope of the present study.

Conclusion

Bonello's essay is an interesting aspect to Maltese constitutional history. The legal historian could find it useful for any light it casts on Malta's medieval "public law"; his political colleague, for the further glimpse it affords on the "emotional reality"[78] in which a segment of nineteenth-century Maltese society couched its self-perception, its perception of its past, and the use of its past – whether real or imagined[79] – as a tool for the negotiation of the future.

---

76 *Ibid. 'In ultima analisi dunque mai e poi mai può avvenire che, salva la giustizia, si possa effettuare il caso in cui il bene privato si possa* realmente *immolaro al pubblico, perchè l'interesse personale* debba *cedere nel volgare significato al pubblico'.*

77 *Ibid. '... per la sola ragione e causa, in cui sia di maggiore interesse privato che il bene dell'individuo, derivante dai rapporti pubblici, venga preferito a quello che deriva dai rapporti puramente privati'.*

78 The felicitous phrase used by Mallia-Milanes, *supra*.

79 Probably more real than imagined.

J.J. Dillon's 1807 *Memoir* on Malta

Appeared in *Melita Historica* XVIII (2021) 2

This essay proposes to highlight some aspects of a British lawyer's memorial published in 1807, that discusses, *inter alia*, the same issue raised by Barry Hough and Howard Davis in their 2007essay 'The British Claim to Rule Malta 1800–1813',[1] namely whether the British acquired sovereignty over Malta through conquest or voluntary-informal cession. While reporting that the Maltese preferred the latter thesis, Hough and Davis point out that the 'British maverick official, William Eton, [...] also argued for cession',[2] but they do not mention Dillon and his *Memoir*.

Sir John Joseph Dillon

A hereditary Knight and Baron of the Holy Roman Empire[3] and a barrister-at-law since 1801,[4] Dillon (*d.*1837)[5] published works on legal and political subjects: the admissibility of Catholics in Parliament (1801), the history and effects of the coronation oath (1807), the Catholic Question (1810), the royal marriage (1811), the conduct of the Administration in Ireland (1812), and the case on the children of the Duke of Sussex (1832).[6]

In his 28-page-long *Memoir Concerning the Political State of Malta* (1807),[7] Dillon sympathises with Maltese views, argues the military and economic importance of Malta to the British Empire, and gives 'reasons (more politely than Eton had done) why Sir Alexander Ball should be replaced'.[8] He also advocates the utility of a constitution for Malta and makes observations on the Maltese.

---

1 Barry Hough, and Howard Davis, (2007), "The British Claim to Rule Malta 1800–1813" in *Melita Historica*, vol. xiv XIV no. 4, Malta: Soċjetà Storika ta' Malta, 387–408. It later appeared as an introductory essay in Lee, H., Hough, B., and Davis, H. (2017) *Constitutional History of Malta 1800-1914*, Oxford: Oxford Legal Publishing, 1–27.

2 *Ibid.*, 21.

3 Coburn, K. (ed.) (2002 [1973]), *The Notebooks of Samuel Taylor Coleridge* Vol. 3: 1808-1819 Notes, Abingdon: Routledge, 4134.

4 Sylvanus Urban (1837) 'Sir John Joseph Dillon' in *The Gentleman's Magazine*, Vol. III, July to December 1837, London: Pickering, 317.

5 *Ibid.*

6 *Ibid.*

7 Dillon, J.J. (1807), *A Memoir concerning the Political State of Malta*, London: Booker.

8 Coburn, 4134.

A satisfactory definition of "constitution", current at more or less the same time Dillon published his *Memoir*, can be found in the anonymous short treatise, *Common Consent, The Basis of the Constitution of England*:[9]

> The constitution is the system of those immemorial rights and antient [*sic*] laws which have reference to the sanction of laws, to the form of government, the powers and duties of the governors, the protection, immunities and duties of the governed, and the means of preserving due order between them.[10]
>
> [...] common consent is the constitutional sanction of our laws [...][11]
>
> [...] it still remains an essential part of the English constitution, that laws ought to be made with the common consent of the whole realm, and that such common consent ought to be expressed in parliament.[12]

Synopsis of Dillon's *Memoir*

The *Memoir* opens with a relatively long dedication to the Duke of Sussex.

The Preface then presents the twin arguments that a constitution for Malta should be written with the Maltese and that Britain had no right to enact laws for the Maltese without their consent.

The points made in Part I are: the importance of Malta to British imperial interests; Britain should not wait for peace to be established before declaring her intention of keeping Malta; without a constitution, the Maltese could resort to violence against the British; the then administrator of Malta, Alexander Ball, should be replaced.

---

9 Anon. (1817), *Common Consent, The Basis of the Constitution of England; or, Parliamentary Reform, Considered and Tried by the Tests of Law and Reason*, London: Allman.

10 *Ibid.*, 16.

11 *Ibid.*, 16–17.

12 *Ibid.*, 24.

The points made in Part II are: should Malta be an independent principality governed by a Prince from the British Royal Family or a dominion?; annexation to the Empire would be better than independence, while assuring overall improvement to the Maltese; the British in Malta were occupants with the permission of the Maltese; the effect of the latter point on the application of English law in Malta.

The *Memoir* ends with legal considerations.

Part I

In Part I, Dillon lays down the premises for the arguments he proposes later, by sharing his admiration for the Maltese, 'a people neither mean nor abject, but resolute and intrepid; [who] know how to wage with success internal war: perhaps no nation ever struggled more strenuously for its liberties.'[13] '[T]heir repeated purchases of the island to themselves' 'in ancient times' and two recent episodes when they showed their 'love of liberty and a wish for independence' (the 1775 Rising of the Priests and the 1798 Insurrection against the French) attest to this.[14] He also *panegyrises* the 'tractability of the Maltese character [that,] inspired with that love of liberty which revolts at oppression, but which in its ardor [*sic*] to regain lost freedom degenerates not into licentiousness[,] shews [*sic*] them to be *capable* of liberty'.[15]

He claims that 'even Charles V. experienced the greatest difficulty in inducing this people to receive the knights'[16] succeeding in convincing them only 'upon a representation of the advantages which would arise to the cause of religion from the establishment of the order in that island, and of the security which would result to themselves against foreign invasion'.[17]Dillon draws parallels with the situation then obtaining between the British and the Maltese:

> As to ourselves we appeared before the island not to make *war upon the Maltese* but to drive out the common foe, whom they also sought to expel. We were only as allies or confederates in a common

13 Dillon, 6.

14 *Ibid.*

15 *Ibid.*, 7.

16 *Ibid.*, 8.

17 *Ibid.*

> undertaking […] and the subsequent submission of the Maltese, or rather their acquiescence in our occupation of the island, can never be considered upon any received principle whatever as that of the vanquished to the conqueror, as of a hostile power to a victorious invader, but as of a free and independent people consenting to sheath the sword, upon and implied and even express assurance that the object, for which they had contended against the French, should be secured by the generous magnanimity of a British sovereign, and under his royal protection, viz. THEIR LIBERTIES AND THEIR LAWS.[18]

He harps on the 'spirit of both liberty and loyalty' that burns within 'a free and gallant nation like the Maltese' and warns against the 'woful [*sic*] mistake' of 'reason[ing] with respect to Malta and its inhabitants upon the same principles as might regulate [British] conduct in the case of a *colony* in the Western world, planted by [the British] or acquired by conquest or treaty from another nation'.[19] He advocates 'a settled form of constitution [to] be speedily adopted' to secure the 'laws and liberties' of the Maltese',[20] continuing that

> at present there exists no constitution in Malta established by law [and] the power of a governor under such circumstances with a numerous garrison at his command, must be of a nature to render it hazardous for persons to transmit, in a minute detailed manner, the nature of their complaints to this country […] excit[ing] in [the Maltese] displeasure and strong prepossessions against the individual entrusted with the government. […] The governor of Malta at present is sole legislator and final judge of his enactments; and no checks according to the existing system in that island are imposed on any improper use of such unlimited authority.[21]

---

18 *Ibid.*, 9–10.

19 *Ibid.*, 10.

20 *Ibid.*, 12.

21 *Ibid.*, 14–15.

Dillon argues that Britain was 'not entitled to enact [laws] for the Maltese, nor would it be wise to adopt such a system, as in the case of other acquisitions.'[22] Common consent is a must for him: 'In any constitution that may be settled for the government of this island the right of the people, through a legislative assembly freely chosen and free in its deliberations, to complain of the conduct of the governor must be effectually secured.'[23] This privilege he reckons must be 'a fundamental principle of the new constitution' that must be 'a system of rational liberty [...] established and secured by law'.[24]

Part II

This part deals with 'the form of government which it may be proper to establish for the island.'[25]

Dillon starts off by asking 'whether the island should be constituted under a prince of the House of Brunswick a separate and independent principality or archduchy; or whether it should form part of the British dominions, as the island of Jersey and Guernsey'.[26] He shoots down his own suggestion and upholds the option of 'annexing the Maltese islands to the imperial dominions of Great Britain'[27] while 'allow[ing] the Maltese the enjoyment perhaps of greater privileges, than are at present held by the natives of other islands under our dependence.'[28]

> The constitution for Malta should 'ke[ep] in view [...] security to the Maltese of liberty, and to Great Britain [...] full power adequate to correct by law the effects, which might result from an abuse of liberty at any time by the Maltese.[29]

He then turns to the matter of drafting a constitution for the Maltese:

22 *Ibid.*, 17.

23 *Ibid.*

24 *Ibid.*

25 *Ibid.*, 21.

26 *Ibid.*

27 *Ibid.*, 22.

28 *Ibid.*, 23.

29 *Ibid.*

> Upon a review of their history it should seem, that in modern times the Maltese have been acquainted with their constitution more in theory than in effect – that during a long period of years they have been totally deprived of the *Consiglio Popolare* – that previously to the year 1775 when that assembly which the Maltese considered as the palladium of their liberties ceased to be convened, its constitution had been perverted – that they had long been debarred from the experience of its effects, and that in 1782 [*sic*] it was formally superseded by the code which was substituted by prince De Rohan. It is difficult to restore to its pristine vigor [*sic*] any constitution that has been long disused; and codes, which have become obsolete or have been during a time abandoned, require much modification when resumed: they are like vestments of the body, the fashion of which when antiquated renders alteration indispensable. Constitutions to be useful must have been continued: that constitution alone is good which has grown with the nation, has varied with the habits of the people and the temper of the times, that which can accommodate itself on all occasions to the circumstances of the country.[30]

'This reasoning,' he opines, 'seems applicable to the state of Malta. *There the sovereignty appears to me to be vacant*, and the change which has taken place in the destiny of the island to require a new constitution, suited to its new situation, and its connection with Great Britain.'[31]

At this point, he brings to the fore what probably constitutes the intention behind this *Memoir*:

> Let then, but by common consent, all existing codes and constitutions be revised, and modified in a manner suitable to the present times. Let a new system comprehending every thing [*sic*] that was

---

30 *Ibid.*

31 *Ibid.*, 24.

> wise – every thing that was free – every thing that is reasonably desired by the Maltese in the laws of former times be introduced; and let the day of its adoption be a new æra [*sic*], from the date of which all former broils shall be forgotten in the establishment of liberty and good government on a solid and permanent basis, ensuring the enjoyment of future tranquillity, of encreasing [*sic*] prosperity, of national exaltation, and of those blessings which the Maltese so eminently deserve, and which they are entitled to claim upon the strongest grounds of justice and good faith from the people of Great Britain.[32]

Dillon approaches the conclusion by referring, albeit fleetingly, to the manner in which Britain possessed Malta, which, he suggests, was 'anomalous in the history of [her] foreign acquisitions'.[33] His advice is that 'the validity of [her] title to the sovereignty of the island' should be beyond the ability of 'the most subtle civilian to dispute', given that the Maltese 'seem a people as far as [the British could] judge from their memorials well versed in the law of nations as it regards usurpation, and disposed to question more the right of the propounder [*sic*], than the merit of the law'.[34]

Considerations of a juridical nature

Finally, Dillon wears the barrister's robe. Had he done so earlier, his underlying plea for a commission might have met with success:

> In countries conquered after defence made, and in the absence of capitulation expressed or implied from the circumstances of the surrender, it is an acknowledged rule that the conqueror is at liberty to change the laws of the country; and by our laws his Majesty's proclamation is binding upon such acquisitions. But surely under the circumstances by which we are in possession of Malta it never can

---

32 *Ibid.*

33 *Ibid.*, 26.

34 *Ibid.*

> be conceived even by ourselves, and certainly not likely to be conceded by the Maltese, that the King's proclamation can have in that island at present any validity, as to prospective and permanent regulations of government – nor could even an act of parliament have greater force.
>
> We must therefore have recourse to the people of Malta for their consent to the enactments we may propose. In other countries such a proceeding might be advisable upon principles of prudence – in Malta it is requisite, upon the ground of INDISPENSABLE NECESSITY. Without their consent we cannot establish a single regulation of a permanent nature. We are SOVEREIGNS of the island only de facto and not de jure. We are neither CONQUERORS, nor PROPRIETORS, nor MORTGAGEES, nor have we any claims of INDEMNITY against this island. We are OCCUPANTS only by PERMISSION of the MALTESE [...]
>
> This I consider clear upon received principles of law, and if it were not, it is absolutely the persuasion of the Maltese, proved by their repeated remonstrances to the British government. Under such circumstances, to transplant there our laws without their free consent and approbation, would be to sow dragons teeth [sic] upon the island [...][35]

We could outline Dillon's argument thus: (1) Malta needs a constitution and new laws, inspired by managed liberty and possibly by Britain's own laws; (2) the drafter needs to know the Maltese people and their character; (3) Dillon is a barrister and happens to know the Maltese; therefore (4) Dillon should be hired to draft a constitution and new laws for this people. In fact, this is how he closes his *Memoir*:

> How then are we to proceed with security in the stability of what may be enacted? I answer like our own ancestors in 1688. An assembly as general as possible may be convened of the inhabitants of

35 *Ibid.*, 27.

> the island [during which] an instrument may be effected similar to our Bill of Rights, and the leading principles of the proposed constitution might be inserted with a preamble [that] might recite the ancient freedom and independence of Malta – the establishment of the knights by Charles V. – the surrender of the knights to the French – the war of the Maltese against the French, and with great delicacy, the surrender of the French to the British forces. It might then proceed to state that the people of Malta, assembled through their representatives, tendered the island and themselves as subjects to his Majesty under the protection of the British empire, upon the conditions therein mentioned, and that his Majesty is graciously pleased to accept the sovereignty of the island and the inhabitants thereof as his subjects accordingly.
>
> By such an act, and by such an act alone can his Majesty obtain a clear indefeasible right to the sovereignty of this island, and the possibility be created of legislating, upon sure principles, for its welfare. Such I am convinced must be the opinion of every jurist upon a review of the circumstances under which we have obtained a footing in Malta so essential to our existence as a great naval power in the Mediterranean.[36]

Contemporary Reactions to the *Memoir*

Whereas I have been unable to find the Duke of Sussex's reaction, assuming there is one, and Alexander Ball's is analysed hereunder, I can nonetheless quote at least two reactions that appeared in print that same year.

The Critical Review disagreed with Dillon 'about the wisdom or the policy of preserving the dominion of the island',[37] because, it argued, '[t]he

---

36 *Ibid.*, 28.

37 (1807) *The Critical Review. Or, Annals of Literature* Series theThird, Vol. XI, London: J. Mawman, 419.

more we conquer from the enemy in other countries, the more liable we become to be conquered in our own'.[38] It did, however, agree with Dillon's constitutional argument: 'If we retain the possession, we entirely agree [...] that we ought to frame such a constitution for the island, as is best suited to the habits, and most agreeable to the wishes of the people'.[39]

The Monthly Review disagreed with Dillon that 'the Crown of Great Britain d[id] not hold Malta as a subject-country, but merely as its protector and ally'.[40] But they did 'assent to the advice which he offer[ed] to ministers, that [Britain] should [...] endeavour to effect that settlement of its government, which may be calculated to conciliate [the Maltese people's] affections, and secure their allegiance'.[41] But this Review was on the whole sceptical as 'the Maltese [we]re all *Catholics*, and they w[ould] want a succession of popish priests [...] and it w[ould] require that [Britain] should act on the principles of catholic emancipation.'[42]

Reason behind the *Memoir*

Why did Dillon write this *Memoir*? Was he acting on behalf of Maltese clients? Did he travel to Malta, or did he meet Maltese activists in London? Or was it the result merely of perusal of printed matter on the Maltese situation?

Alexander Ball dismissed Dillon's (and Eton's) books in a letter dated August 2, 1807:

> Mr. Eton and Mr. Dillon have lately published two books on Malta tending to prejudice me in the public mind and to get me removed from the situation, that they and their friends may come here and direct the administration under the Duke of Sussex. I have answered Mr. Eton's charges [...][43]

---

38 *Ibid.*, 420.

39 *Ibid.*, 419.

40 (1807) *The Monthly Review, or Literary Journal of England* Vol. LIV, London: Becket, 97.

41 *Ibid.*

42 *Ibid.*

43 Quoted in Hardman, W. (1909), *A History of Malta, during the period of the French and British occupations 1798–1815*, Part 2, London: Longmans, Green,

Ball does not mention any reply to Dillon.

I am not convinced by Ball's explanation. Some aspects of the *Memoir* would seem to suggest that Dillon was seeking a commission to draft a constitution or 'code of laws' for Malta. From a passage found elsewhere, it seems reasonable to infer that despite his awareness of the hesitancy and anxiety inherent to the civil service, he failed to address them in a manner conducive to earning him enough trust and the coveted commission: the *Memoir* trespasses on the minefield of internal civil service politics. Dillon's anger and frustration are self-evident in this excerpt from the aforesaid work, published four years later:

> In 1807 I had occasion to publish a Memoir upon the political state of Malta, in the hopes of pressing upon the attention of Ministers the necessity of an immediate settlement to that Island. I was never requested even to communicate the grounds on which I expressed the strong opinions manifested in that publication, still less any idea that might have occurred to me, after a very laborious attention to the subject, respecting the form of constitution or code of laws, suitable to the connection of that Island with the British Empire. I had personally, no pretension to consideration; but the Maltese were entitled to claim the performance of good faith on the part of Britain. Nothing has been done – and it appears that the patience of the Maltese has become nearly exhausted. It is my intention to resume the consideration of the Maltese question.[44] Malta has been sacrificed to the prejudices of ministers regarding Ireland, and nothing has been done for Malta, because it would have afforded an argument for the settlement of Ireland!!![45]

---

and Co., 498.

[44] I have not managed to find anything that demonstrates that he went through with this.

[45] John Joseph Dillon (1811), *The Letters of Hibern-Anglus, containing Strictures on the conduct of the Present Administration in Ireland, and a Vindication of the Proceedings adopted since the Regency by the Irish Catholics, With Other Pa-*

The three exclamation marks at the end give away the author's emotional state. More importantly, the phrase 'I had personally, no pretension to consideration' and its place (following an oblique reference to the drafting of a constitution or a code of laws) clearly suggest that Dillon wrote the *Memoir* in the hope of eliciting a commission.

Dillon's rant is actually a footnote appended to the end of this paragraph:

> One would have thought that the loss of America, principally attributable to the folly of considering not what it was proper to grant, but the grounds on which, what was admitted to be expedient, should be conceded, would have been a warning to the present Administration, and have induced them to deprecate a similar discussion with the people of Ireland. But by a fatality which has so long marked the Proceedings of Great Britain towards her colonies and dependencies, as well as foreign powers, her ministers first oppose every request, however reasonable – repudiate solicitation – promise after a time, and then retard performance – yield at length only to remonstrate – and defeat every advantage resulting from measures, which from the beginning may have been pronounced by men even of ordinary capacity to be of obvious policy. What has been the conduct of the present Administration, for instance, towards Malta?[46]

One intuits that instead of promoting himself as the legal expert the administrators needed to solve their problems, Dillon found himself conveying the unintended impression that he could be a busybody who pokes his nose in administrative affairs, somebody civil servants would not be too keen on getting involved with.

Coda: the Duke of Sussex

In the Dedication, made to the Duke of Sussex, Dillon eulogises the

---

pers, London: Ridgway, and Booker, xxi-xxii.

46 *Ibid.*, xxi.

King's son for his 'enlarged view of the policy which dictates the necessity not only of maintaining, but of extending the influence of the British Empire in the Mediterranean', his 'exertions on a former occasion in impressing upon others a due regard to the importance of Malta', and 'his intimate knowledge of the advantages which, under a judicious settlement of its government, it is capable of affording to this country even in times of peace'.[1]

Dillon whets the Duke's appetite by hinting that the Duke (a member of the House of Brunswick) take over Malta as his own independent principality. Then, in a move that defies rational analysis, Dillon enumerates the reasons why this (unsolicited?) idea should be put aside (thereby seemingly contradicting Ball's possibly spurious accusation).

But the Dedication piques our interest for another reason. The Duke, who, according to Dillon, was remarkably knowledgeable about Malta, had an intimae friendship with Waller Rodwell Wright,[2] the future President of the Court of Appeal in Malta. Among other things, Wright advised the Duke when the two feuding factions within English Freemasonry made peace and created the United Grand Lodge of England in 1813.[3] The Duke of Sussex was one of the factions' Grand Master while his brother, the Duke of Kent, was Grand Master of the other. When the Articles of Union were signed and ratified in 1813,[4] Wright was one of the signatories on behalf of the Duke of Sussex's faction.[5]

Was Wright's appointment in Malta related to the Duke's interest in these islands?

---

1 Dillon, *Dedication.*

2 Wright, D. (rev.) (1936), *Gould'sHistory Of Freemasonry Throughout The World*, Vol. 3, New York: Charles Scribner's Sons, 282.

3 Bogdan, H., & Snoek, J.A.M. (2014), 'The History of Freemasonry: An Overview', in Bogdan, H., & Snoek, J.A.M. (ed.), *Handbook of Freemasonry*, Leiden/Boston: Brill, 13–32, 18-19.

4 Belton, J. (2012), *The English Masonic Union of 1813: A Tale Antient and Modern*, Bury St Edmonds, Suffolk: Arima Publishing, 87.

5 Oliver, G. (1867), *The Origin of the Royal Arch Order of Masonry Historically Considered*, London: Spencer, 66-67.

Constitutional Law as History

Presented during

History Week 2023 titled
The Paths to Independence: Transitions & Transformations (1914-1964)
organised by the Malta Historical Society
November 2023

Malta's constitutional history from 1914 to 1964 (but also before that period) is a series of transitions and transformations. However, I do not intend this as Whiggery. I assert by way of premise that the transformations in the constitutional law of Malta as colony impacted Maltese history, both pre- and post-Independence, in a way that does not denote inevitable progress.

Between 1914 and 1964, Britain gave Malta six constitutions (in 1921, 1936, 1939, 1947, 1959, 1961) – the 1964 Independence Constitution was the seventh. A progressive narrative can be easily spun from this: that these constitutions were transitions marked by improvement, not necessarily in the legal text but in the natives' capability to govern themselves. I disagree with such a Whiggish approach, based on the consideration that the idea of the Empire's civilising mission was nothing more than self-serving and self-justifying propaganda. Instead, in this paper I shall present the hypothesis that the succession of constitutional documents imposed by Britain on Malta imbued the Maltese with cynicism with respect to such documents and possibly to the very idea of *grundnorm*. More importantly, however, I shall argue that the British defective understanding of the modern State contaminated the Maltese mind. Constitutional law thus made history, and keeps making it, as it is in turn itself molded by history. After all, constitutional law is an 'amalgam of law, politics and history'.[1]

What are we meaning by "Constitution"?

A good definition may be borrowed from a book on Malta's 1974 *fraude à la constitution,* when the constitutional monarchy setup was replaced with the Republic. The Constitution can be understood

> above all not as a set of rules, but rather as the relationship of those rules with the sentiments of the community, expressed through the political formations present and operating in Parliament, which thus seek to interpret the new needs of a society in which constitutional rules and values are perceived as having been overtaken by events.[2]

---

1 David, Clark, 'Cautious Constitutionalism: Commonwealth Legislative Independence and the Statute of Westminster 1931-1942', 4 (2016) 16 *Macquarie Law Journal* 41, 42.

2 ['*soprattutto non come insieme di norme, ma piuttosto come il rapporto di quelle regole con i sentimenti della comunità, espressi attraverso le formazioni politiche presenti ed operanti in Parlamento, che cercano così di farsi interpreti*

This definition goes beyond the constitutional document, which is but an instrument of the Constitution itself. A Constitution may be written or unwritten – Britain's is unwritten. And yet, as observed by Dame Linda Colley, '[a]lthough Britain has no written constitution, British lawyers, civil servants, and diplomats have been conspicuously active in writing constitutions for other countries'.[3]

There are at least two ways of looking at a Constitution. Either one views it – almost in Hegelian terms ('The State is the Divine Idea as it exists on Earth') – as a set of universal principles that each country interprets and applies in its own way. Or else, as the result of the organic evolution of a country's history. The latter interpretation is a strand of functionalist thought[4] according to which the British common-law tradition is one of converting history into law.

Whose history?

The British Constitution is the result of the historical evolution of British politics. As Sir Ivor Jennings[5] put it,

> The English jurist is not a sociologist; he is a lawyer, but he has been taught that he cannot be a lawyer unless he is also a historian. For all law (except of course the largest part of it which, being in legislation, tends to be ignored) is simply the scum left by the receding tide of history.[6]

For the British the constitution is 'something which evolves'.[7] As a

delle nuove esigenze di una società nella quale le regole ed i valori costituzionali si avvertono come superati dagli eventi'] – Antonella Cesarini (2001), *Una rivoluzione in forma di legge: Malta 1974 storia di una anomala revisione costituzionale*, Padua: CEDAM, 53.

3 Linda Colley (2014), *Acts of Union and Disunion: What has held the UK together and what has divided it?*, London: Profile Books, 143.

4 Martin Loughlin (1992), *Public Law and Political Theory*, Oxford: Clarendon Press, 167-176.

5 (1903-1965)

6 Ivor Jennings, 'A plea for utilitarianism', (1938) 2 *Modern Law Review* 22, 27-28.

7 Noel Cox, 'The Theory of Sovereignty and the Importance of the Crown in the Realms of the Queen', *Oxford University Commonwealth Law Journal*, 2 (2) 2002, 237-55, 250.

consequence of this evolutionary process, Britain's constitutional 'theory is sometimes developed subsequent to the practice.'[8] This unusual situation (unusual when compared to the civil-law jurisdictions, that is) has meant that English law is marked by the failure to 'develop a coherent theory of state'[9] or 'a general theory of the State'[10]. This, I claim, has had a direct bearing on Maltese history, and on why the Maltese do (or did) not really observe the constitutional document. But about this, later.

For the moment, let us zero in on *whose* history it is, a question that necessitates a broader understanding of "Britain", as '[t]he egress of the British constitution was the constitution of the British Empire; which in turn became an ingress into British constitutional theory.'[11] As one author very recently put it, '[t]he British constitution has always been an imperial constitution.'[12]

Again, we need to look at definitions. What was the "British Empire"?

Already in the late 1500s, 'England was just one nation within the new empire of the *British Iles* (the term is first recorded in 1577). Elizabeth Tudor was no mere English queen. She was a multi-national Empress who wore *the Imperiall Crown*.'[13] The Constitution of England – the precursor of the Constitution of Britain ('the principles of the British Constitution are substantially the same that grew up in England as the principles of the English Constitution'[14]) – was already an *imperial* constitution even before

---

8 Cox, *ibid.*

9 Cris Shore, 'The Crown as Metonym for the State?: The Human Face of Leviathan', in C. Shore and D. Williams (eds.), *The Shapeshifting Crown: Locating the State in Postcolonial New Zealand, Australia, Canada and the UK*, 53–74 (Cambridge: Cambridge University Press 2019), 53.

10 Cox, *ibid.*

11 Coffey, 209.

12 Coel Kirkby (2003), 'The Making of Empire', in Peter Cane & Harshan Kumarasingham (eds), *The Cambridge Constitutional History of the United Kingdom: The Changing Constitution*, Cambridge: Cambridge University Press, 468-495, 468.

13 James Hawes (2021), *The Shortest History of England*, Exeter: Old Street Publishing, 116.

14 Sir Edward Creasy (1872), *The Imperial and Colonial Constitutions of the Britannic Empire*, London, Longmans, Green, and Co., 8.

Britain acquired sovereignty on overseas territories. This sovereignty on overseas territories – the "British Empire", that 'whole aggregate of territory, the inhabitants of which, under various forms of government ultimately look to the British crown as the supreme head'[15] – was 'an historic growth, corresponding to *no* principle[. T]he application of any principle whatever to it would at once torpedo it.'[16]

The British Constitution is thus an amalgamated product of English, and later British history, and the history of the Empire. The Empire was defined by '[m]ultiple and contradictory forms of sovereignty [...] as the different idioms evolved in contrast and opposition to one another.'[17] Imperial history impacted the British Constitution but since '[i]ncoherence and plural sovereignty defined the empire as a political field and historical entity'[18], that impact was even more multi-layered and multi-dimensional than one might be led to believe basing oneself only on the 'effort to tell a coherent and unified story' about the Empire made by late nineteenth-century British universities in their quest to achieve the 'professionalisation of the interrelated fields of history, law and politics'.[19]

The British Constitution can thus be viewed as a complex unwritten understanding among the members of the Metropolitan political class formed by a (wittingly or unwittingly) selective knowledge of English and (later) British history and Imperial histories. Imperial London justifiably feared imperial fragmentation.[20] In response to this risk, Albert Venn Dicey[21] elaborated the doctrine of parliamentary supremacy which 'recognised the unequal power relations which existed between different territories, and then suggested that only a single, central legislative body could bind the disparate communities of empire together'.[22]

---

15 *Encyclopædia Britannica,* 1911 edition, s.v. 'British Empire'.

16 Israel Zangwill (1917), *The Principle of Nationalities,* London: Watts & Company, 34.

17 Jon Wilson and Andrew Dilley (2023), 'The Incoherence of Empire, Or, the Pitfalls of Ignoring Sovereignty in the History of the British Empire', *Transactions of the Royal Historical Society* 1 (2023), 191-217, 194.

18 Wilson et, 194

19 *Ibid.*

20 Wilson et, 194-195.

21 (1835-1922)

22 Wilson et, 195.

This complex constitutional setup became the inspiration for the so-called Westminster model. S.A. de Smith[23] comments that,

> [i]n its widest sense [this model] may be understood to comprise all the main features of the British constitution. [...] In its narrower sense [...] the Westminster model can be said to mean a constitutional system in which the head of state is not the effective head of government; in which the effective head of government is a Prime Minister presiding over a Cabinet composed of Ministers over whose appointment and removal he has at least substantial measure of control; in which the effective executive branch of government is parliamentary inasmuch as Ministers must be members of the legislature; and in which Ministers are collectively and individually responsible to a freely elected and representative legislature.[24]

'The conversion of History into Law' – Sir Ivor Jennings

The British Constitution is a product of historical and political developments not theoretical legal reasoning. In 1960, Jennings delivered a lecture (to which audience we do not know), titled *The Conversion of History into Law,* outlining England's political (or constitutional) history, from the Norman conquest of 1066, to the Magna Charta, to the conflict between Church and State resolved when Henry VIII put the Church under royal control, to the Civil War.

Jennings observed that 'no clear theory came out of the conflict between Church and State [...] The lawyers were royal officers, whose task was merely to determine what were the king's rights and duties, not to reason why.'[25] 'There was not, and there has never been,' he explicitly stated,

> conscious planning either of the common law or of political institutions. There was an immediate problem to be solved, and it received a pragmatic solution. Moreover, the branch

23 (1922-1974)

24 S.A. de Smith (1964), *The New Commonwealth and its Constitutions,* London: Stevens &Sons, 77-78.

25 H. Kumarasingham (2016), 'Sir Ivor Jennings' "The Conversion of History into Law"', *American Journal of Legal History,* 2016, 56, 113–127, 118.

> of history with which I am, as a constitutional lawyer, most concerned, i.e. constitutional history, is a somewhat misleading subject of study. It traces institutions through the morass of political controversy. It therefore picks out the institutions which have evolved and gives them a fictitious importance because they have evolved, whereas the mass of temporary past expedients which had no future are perhaps just mentioned and then put aside. [... I]t is a selection of material based upon a scale of values determined by future developments.[26]

Jennings further explained the historical process leading to the creation of law based on practice:

> Developments occur, always pragmatically. One step is taken to meet an immediate practical need. A little later there is a second practical need: and if that can be solved by repeating or extending the precedent already set a second step is taken. This process continues until a claim of right is established. [...] Where the process is merely an accumulation of precedents, there is a minimum of theorising. Only where there is a conflict over the next step are theories produced. [...] When the age of conflict is over, however, English pragmatism is restored. Moreover the conflict seldom ranges over the whole field of politics, and so there is never any need to produce a complete political theory.[27]
>
> [...T]he essence of the pragmatic method is that slow evolution wraps our institutions in the fabric of society. It is a process of adapting institutions to new needs, and all social institutions are adapted together with very little of conscious planning. [...] Moreover, slow evolution implies that there can be evolution and not revolution. Evolution has been possible in Britain because it was a small island, difficult to invade because of the weather, and provided with excellent harbours which gave access to an expanding

26 *Ibid.*, 124.

27 *Ibid.*, 126.

> world. No doubt there were other accidental advantages which kept it out of the dynastic squabbles of Europe and enabled it to overcome the dangers of the 15th and 17th centuries.[28]

In other words, the constitutional law of Britain – the land where, coincidentally (?), Darwinism was born and bred – is the result of accident not design.

The lecture's parting shot reflected Jennings's role as a constitutional consultant: 'Even, so, the problem remains. How can British institutions be transplanted to Nigeria and made to flourish there?'[29] Nigeria acquired independence from Britain on 1 October 1960, the same year the lecture was delivered.

Is Malta another Nigeria?

In the context of this essay, we should be intellectually amused at the mention of Nigeria: Malta's 1964 Constitution is a 'modified version of the Nigerian model'.[30] (The 1961 Constitution too had featured a "neo-Nigerian" characteristic: an enforceable Bill of Rights.[31])

Jennings's lecture's parting shot turned out to be prophetic. In 1979, Nigeria abandoned the Westminster model for a new constitution, inspired by the American or 'Washington' model. The 'transition from the Westminster to a Washington model [wa]s a logical, predictable one'.[32]

The Maltese have never formally departed from the Westminster model. Then again, one has to ask – and this is the second central question of this essay – whether the Maltese have really embraced the Westminster model as expressed in Malta's constitutional document.

Let us pause, to find our bearings. There are two central, inter-related questions in this essay. One: can a country's constitution, produced by the

---

28 *Ibid.*, 126-27.

29 *Ibid.*, 127.

30 de Smith, 193.

31 J.J. Cremona (1994), *The Maltese Constitution and Constitutional History since 1813*, Malta: PEG, 69.

32 James R Read (1979), 'The New Constitution of Nigeria, 1979: "The Washington Model"?', *Journal of African Law*, 23 (1979) 2, 131-174, 131.

history of that country, be transplanted to another country? Two: have the Maltese really embraced a constitutional document framed not according to their history but to the multi-dimensional history of their colonial masters?

Even a cursory scansion of Malta's political history indicates that the transplant has been only partially successful: the Maltese do not really follow their written constitution. Expressed in "legalese": 'The Constitution's weak entrenchment is embedded within the document's legal provisions, and the political, conventional, and judicial practices of the constitutional system leaves this much unchanged.'[33]

Consider: Malta's Constitution contemplates the Prime Minister as a *primus inter pares* ("first among equals") appointed by the President of Malta among sitting Members of Parliament. Article 80 of the constitutional document *clearly* lays down that 'the President shall appoint as Prime Minister the member of the House of Representatives who, in his judgment, is best able to command the support of a majority of the members of that House'. But this is not how things are done on the ground. In reality, the President's judgment is but an acknowledgement of political party practice (though, admittedly, this in itself could be a constitutional convention): parties elect their Leaders, through internal party mechanisms that seem bereft of any public-law dimension – internal party affairs are not regulated by the Constitution. The Prime Minister of Malta is a sort of Prince of Malta, a *Princeps* more than a *Primus,* not too distant from the notion of "Prince" explained by Antonio Micallef in his lectures on the Government of the Order of Saint John (Micallef compared the Prince-Grand Master to Moses, 'the true and effective monarch of the Jewish People'[34]). An Absolute Prince, as the *Uditore* Niccolò Muscat[35] had in mind when he argued against the introduction of judicial precedent in Malta proposed by Giandonato Rogadeo, the Naples-trained lawyer engaged by Grand Master de Rohan to reform the Maltese legal and judicial systems.[36] However, Professor

---

33 John Stanton (2019), 'The Constitution of Malta: Supremacy, Parliament and Separation of Powers', 6 (2019) I *JICL* 47-73, 56.

34 Antonio Micallef (2012 [1792]), *Lectures on the Statutes of the Sacred Order of St. John of Jerusalem at the University of Malta 1792* (tr. Michael Galea),Karlsruhe: KIT Scientific Publishing, 49.

35 (1735-c. 1800)

36 Niccolò Muscat (1783), *Apologia a Favore dell'Inclita Nazione Maltese,* Malta, 95-96.

Guglielmo Rapinet[37], in 1883, explained to his law students that the British government was a 'Party Government'.[38] There is nothing written in the 1964 Constitution of Malta hinting at this constitutional infrastructure, and yet the Maltese follow it nonetheless.

(Malta's Constitution does take into consideration the Leaders of parties, but only with regard to the appointment of the Leader of the Opposition. Article 90 lays down that 'whenever there shall be occasion for the appointment of a Leader of the Opposition, the President shall appoint - (a) if there is one opposition party whose numerical strength in the House of Representatives is greater than the strength of any other opposition party, the member of the House of Representatives who is the Leader of that party'.)

Another example is the Cabinet presided upon by the Prime Minister. This is not due to theoretical considerations, but only because the Maltese follow the English system which came into being since King George I, being German, could not speak English and therefore, unlike his predecessors, did not attend Cabinet meetings.[39] This historical development became part and parcel of the British Constitution, and was then passed on to Malta, without there being any rationale why the Maltese should follow this principle conceived out of something as mundane as the Monarch's linguistic limitations except that that was what the former colonial master did.

It can thus be argued there seems to be two parallel dichotomies in Malta: (1) between a theoretical Westminster model and practice conceived on lines perhaps similar to how the Knights of St John managed their constitutional affairs, and (2) British constitutional principles which were not transposed to the written Westminster-model Constitution of Malta.

There seems to be a substratum of Maltese indigenous law which steadfastly refuses elimination. This substratum is a legacy of the colonial policy to preserve colonies as they had been found except when it suited the Empire to develop them. As Rapinet explains in his Constitutional Law course, there was

> a faint reproduction of the British Government in the

---

37 (1843-1912), Professor of Constitutional Law and Economics.

38 Guglielmo Rapinet (1883), Lectures on the British Constitution and on the Government of Malta, Malta: Aquilina, 76.

39 Rapinet, 79.

> administrative and legislative organization of Malta. [...] These differences between the model and the copy are due, mainly, [...] to [the fact] that in dependencies, which are garrison towns and naval stations, imperial interests are supreme; and that in territories acquired by cession, and inhabited by a different and civilized race, the existing laws and customs of the people are retained until the native population is gradually prepared to appreciate and use the franchises of Englishmen.[40]

Rapinet's text justifies Homi Bhabha's concept of 'colonial mimicry'[41]: 'from the perspective of the colonizer, the colonized must be sufficiently similar to be "civilizable", but sufficiently different to justify domination'.[42]

It would also explain why the British Governors perpetuated the style of the Grand Masters, as further confirmed by this other excerpt when Rapinet analyses the 'conduct of the French during their short-lived possession of Malta in 1798':[43]

> The French introduced in the island, immediately on assuming the administration of its government, and without any regard to the ancient institutions of the monastic Order, which they dispossessed, all the modern laws of revolutionary France [...] The inhabitants rose in insurrection, and expelled the would-be reformers.[44]

The "constitutional law" of the Order seems to have been retained as a precautionary measure, to avoid insurrection.

Despite the word and spirit of the 1964 Constitution, the Maltese – acting in the way analysed by Martti Koskenniemi in his works – perpetuated the style of the Governors. Then again, this would not be unique: 'African

---

40 Rapinet, 208.

41 H.K. Bhabha (1994), *The Location of Culture*, London: Routledge, 121-131.

42 Andrew Lang & Susan Marks (2017), 'Even the Dead Will Not Be Safe', in (Wouter Werner *et*, eds.), *The Law of International Lawyers: Reading Martti Koskenniemi*, 321–339, 329.

43 Rapinet, 144.

44 Rapinet, 144.

presidents replaced their colonial governors in fact and in deed. Like the colonial governors, they became the sole embodiment of the social will and purposes of the countries they ruled.'[45]

A question of attitudes

The British could accommodate contradictions because their Constitution is unwritten. When a constitution is written (and, in many cases, therefore also rigid), however, it is either obeyed or else it is amended through positive legislative action (even though, in theory at least, 'a rigid Constitution is thought of as a Constitution which, because it contains legal obstacles, is hard to alter and is seldom altered'[46]). A written constitution cannot simply be ignored and left unapplied. So much so that a written constitution has to be 'drafted very clearly to avoid confusion in the minds of actors who would naturally look to the wording of the constitution rather than the extensive and sometimes debatable constitutional history and understanding that led to it'.[47] This is probably the reason why 'dominions [had] the proclivity towards written constitutions'.[48]

Why does this attitude prevail in Malta? I suggest that the reasons are (at least) two.

The first is due to 'misunderstanding the constitution'.[49] I concur with the opinion already articulated and published that the Maltese have kept faithful to the British Constitution proper rather than embracing the constitutional document the British gave them. The Maltese embrace an

---

45 Muna Ndulo, 'Constitutions and Constitutional Reforms in African Politics', https://oxfordre.com/politics/display/10.1093/acrefore/9780190228637.001.0001/acrefore-9780190228637-e-1324 (accessed 1 November 2023).

46 K.C. Wheare (1966), *Modern Constitutions*, Oxford: Oxford University Press, 17.

47 A. Harding, (2004) 'The Westminster Model Constitution Overseas' (2004) 4 *Oxford University Commonwealth Law J.*, 4 (2004) 2, 156.

48 Donal K. Coffey (2020), "Constitutional law and empire in interwar Britain: universities, liberty, nationality and parliamentary supremacy", *Northern Ireland Legal Quarterly* 71 (2020) 2, 193-209, 200.

49 A nod to a extraordinary book penned by Giovanni Bonello (*Misunderstanding the Constitution: How the Maltese judiciary undermines human rights,* Malta: BDL 2018). When I reviewed it (*The Malta Independent on Sunday,* March 12, 2019), I hailed it as 'the most important book of the decade'. My opinion has not wavered.

attitude that 'appears reminiscent of the United Kingdom's own constitutional arrangement – from which Malta sought to separate in the 1960s – in recognising the supremacy of Parliament, rather than the supremacy of the Constitution, even when prevailing constitutional provisions and norms would seem to support the latter over the former.'[50]

This attitude was best captured by former President of the Constitutional Court Giuseppe Mifsud Bonnici,[51] during a public debate that also involved Giovanni Bonello (former European Court of Human Rights judge) and Silvio Camilleri (then President of the Constitutional Court) in 2012 and 2013:

> Supremacy is a question of power. Where lies the ultimate power in our state? With us there is no doubt it is Parliament that has the power to do whatever it wills with a two-thirds majority of its members. Our Constitution was modelled on the lines of the British "Constitution" and there Parliament is supreme. And so it is with us, the only difference being that, in our case, that supremacy is watered down by the two-thirds majority rule ... Nevertheless, Parliament is supreme – not the Constitution.[52]

However, this reasoning applies to an *imperial* not a *national* constitution. Dicey had the governability of the Empire in mind, not a small island-nation.

This aspect of post-Independence Malta is possibly due to the country's pre-Independence constitutional history, with its many transitions and transformations when constitutional documents were given to and taken from the Maltese almost as if constitutions were toys – whereas 'the very act of enunciating a constitution [should] mark a historic rupture'.[53]

There were too many "ruptures" in Maltese constitutional history, none of them truly historic. This almost whimsical (but obviously politically

---

50 Stanton, 73.

51 (1930-2019)

52 Giuseppe Mifsud Bonnici, 'The Supremacy of Parliament', *The Times of Malta*, 2 June 2012.

53 U. Baxi (2000), 'Postcolonial Legacy' in *A Companion to Postcolonial Studies* (H. Schwarz and S. Ray eds.), Oxford: Blackwell, 540-555, 541.

expedient) approach to constitutional documents must have left an indelible mark on the Maltese psyche: constitutional documents perceived as nothing more than pieces of paper that come and go according to the moment's political expediencies. In a sense – but only in *a* sense – this series of "ruptures" reflected British legal culture: since the British constitution is unwritten, its contents can evolve without too much formality. The British could therefore afford avoiding having to come to terms with the implications of a written constitution and with the formalities on which such documents depend for their validity in the eyes of all political actors, be they those who govern or are governed. This flexible attitude must have impacted the Maltese, for whom the Constitution is not what continental Europeans understand it to be.

Whereas for the British the British Constitution was the result of historical development, for the Maltese the same British Constitution (or its derivative) was the result of ideology – the ideology of imperialism and its flaunted civilising mission.

There are two aspects to the proclamation of a constitution: 'the political process through which a constitution is made, and the legal contents of the document'.[54] For the British their Constitution evolved in the typical common-law fashion, that is to say bottom-up; for the Maltese, the British Constitution (or its derivative) was created in the typical civil-law fashion, that is to say top-down: the handing down of concepts and rules by a higher authority. Such Mount-Sinai-like events can have long-lasting effects only if the rules emanate from an authority considered divine. (Again, Hegel's philosophy on the State comes to mind.)

More on attitudes

Jennings argued that 'the British constitutional framework is ultimately guaranteed, in Lockean terms, by the people's right to rebel against tyranny.'[55] He argued that 'the key British constitutional tenet of parliamentary supremacy, while a recognized principle of the common law, was not established in Britain by judicial decision'[56] but as a result of the English Revolution and the Glorious Revolution. Jennings believed that

---

54 Mara Malagodi (2015), 'Ivor Jennings' Constitutional Legacy beyond the Occidental-Oriental Divide', *Journal of Law and Society*, 42 (2015) 1, 102-126, 118.

55 *Ibid.*, 105.

56 *Ibid.*, 105-06.

'liberty in Britain is grounded in the spirit of a free people, who took up arms and fought for "freedom for a reformed Church, freedom from royal absolutism, parliamentary freedom".'[57] One can see where Jennings is coming from. Just consider that in 1910, Malta's colonial administration proposed an Ordnance (later withdrawn) 'to regulate the right to carry arms even in one's own house by making it subject to a police licence, – a measure that was shown to be at odds with the sacrosanct right of self-defence.'[58] On that occasion the colonial administration had sensed correctly – only nine years later, on 7 June 1919, the Maltese rose, and the uprising eventually paved the way for the 1921 Constitution. The Maltese proved Jennings right when he wrote that 'liberty is an attitude of the mind'.[59]

However, uprisings against tyranny are costly; constitutional setups with in-built legal (i.e., non-violent) antidotes to "tyrants" are more conducive to stability and the creation of wealth. England did go through a period of violence, followed by a constitutional solution: 'the prerogative powers of the Crown were at one time personal powers of the Sovereign; and it was only by slow degrees that they were converted to the use of the real executive body, and so brought under control of Parliament.'[60] During the English Civil War, the Crown and Parliament wrestled for sovereignty. The Royalists asserted the divine rights of Kings 'to reign irrespective of the consent of the people';[61] the Parliamentarians articulated 'new historical arguments about England's "ancient constitution" based on sovereignty of parliament since time immemorial.'[62] Then, the 'rise of Robert Walpole signalled the beginnings of a form of Cabinet government led by a strong first minister asserting the rights and privileges of Parliament against the Crown'.[63] (And, as we have seen, King George's linguistic knowledge, or to be more accurate, lack of it.)

---

57 *Ibid.*, 106.

58 Arturo Mercieca (1969), *The Making and Unmaking of a Maltese Chief Justice*, Malta: Giov. Muscat, 91.

59 Ivor Jennings (1966), *The British Constitution,* Cambridge: Cambridge University Press (5th ed.), 203.

60 P. Cobbett (1904), 'The Crown as Representing the State', *Commonwealth Law Review,* 1 (1904) 4, 145-156, 146.

61 Alfred O'Rahilly (1922), 'Allegiance and the Crown', *An Irish Quarterly Review,* 11 (1922) 42, 169-185, 174.

62 Kirkby, 474.

63 Kirkby, 480.

Then, Jennings suggested, against the power of Parliament there is the 'attitude of mind' and the 'spirit of a free people' ready to rise up in arms. But a constitutional document that functions properly becomes the voice of the people against Parliament's possible abuses of power. Not for nothing does the American Constitution's Preamble open with the formula, '*We the People* of the United States, in Order to form a more perfect Union, establish Justice, *insure domestic Tranquility*, provide for the common defense, promote the general Welfare, and secure the Blessings of Liberty to ourselves and our Posterity, *do ordain and establish this Constitution* for the United States of America' [emphasis added].

The Maltese could decide to start understanding their Constitution from this American perspective, accepting the constitutional document as embodiment of the People and serving as the People's shield against Parliament. Instead, it is submitted, on account of the vacuous constitutional transitions and transformations of the pre-Independence period, the Maltese stubbornly follow the British Constitution proper, which, technically, is not the blueprint for Malta's Constitution. This blind adherence to the teachings of scholars rather than to the text is, I submit, commonplace in Malta, as I have argued elsewhere.[64] It is also commonplace among former British colonies in Africa: 'Independence did not change the fundamental structure of the colonial society [...] In almost all cases, the African independence leadership took over the colonial state as established by the departing colonial power.'[65]

With this blind allegiance to a foreign model that has no local legal standing, the Maltese have also acquiesced to 'the absence of a developed legal notion of the state as a "sovereign community"'.[66] Indeed, 'the State is an entity unknown to [English] law'.[67] This lacuna in British legal theory has prompted scholars even to claim that '[i]n the British system and those derived from it, it is questionable whether there is a State.'[68]

---

64 *Vide* 'Judicial Importation into Maltese Law of Italian Private Law: Solutions and Its Implications' in Mark A. Sammut (2017), *Essays in Maltese Legal History and Comparative Law*, Oxford: OLP, 3-17.

65 Ndulo

66 Cheryl Saunders (2015), 'The Concept of the Crown', *Melbourne University Law Review*, 38 (2015), 873-896, 876.

67 O'Rahilly, 176.

68 Noel Cox (2002), 'The Theory of Sovereignty and the Importance of the Crown in the Realms of the Queen', *Oxford University Commonwealth Law Journal*, 2 (2002) 2, 237-55, 251.

Conclusion

All said and done, the period from 1914 to 1964 does not really have much to show in terms of transitions and transformations in mentality. Despite the wording of the 1964 Constitution, the Maltese keep following the British Constitution proper, possibly unaware that its underpinnings depend on Britain's history which Malta does not share. Formal transitions ("new" constitutional documents) did not translate into material transformations (new mentalities). Even the 1974 *fraude à la constitution* was but a positivist rendition of the *de facto* situation obtaining in Britain, since 'on any scientific classification England would rank as a republic'.[1]

Constitutional law has determined Maltese history. 'Nigeria is a creation of the Constitution'[2] but perhaps so is Malta. As Carmel Vassallo put it, 'We have to accept that Malta is indeed a "creation of empire".'[3] The question now becomes: What shall we do next? Shall we transition and transform on the occasion of the sixtieth anniversary of Independence? From *Malta's* Constitution to the *Maltese* Constitution?

---

1 O'Rahilly, 181.

2 Sam Eleanya, *Nigeria: Constitutional Development and History* https://constitution.lawnigeria.com/2018/03/26/nigeria-constitution-development-and-history/ (accessed 1 November 2023).

3 Carmel Vassallo (2003), 'A nationless state or a stateless nation', *The Times of Malta*, February 9, 2003.

REVIEWS

Understanding Giovanni Bonello: The Most Important Book of the Decade

The Malta Independent
March 12, 2019

I think it is self-evident that Giovanni Bonello's *Misunderstanding the Constitution: How the Maltese Judiciary Undermines Human Rights* (BDL, 2018, 190 pp.) is the most important book of the decade.

It is admittedly a small book. It has the same size usually reserved for poetry books. But neither size nor cover have ever been a good indicator of the quality of a book's contents. This book is for Malta what the books of the *philosophes* were for France. The *philosophes* were the French intellectuals who opened the eyes of the French middle classes to the abuses perpetrated by the system and how a better France could be carved out of the old one. They paved the way for France to become Modern.

Modernity's greatest achievement has not been democracy in the sense of the ruled (s)electing the rulers or empowering them to rule (this had already been achieved one way or another during the ages). Modernity's greatest achievement consists in the checks and balances meant to limit the power of rulers and their servants. In other words, the shift from the rule *of men* to the rule *of law*.

This book is an invitation to the thinking public to discard the absolutist conception of the State which we still collectively and neurotically cling to. The thinking public is invited to embrace the modern vision of the State as a vehicle for the individual's well-being and self-fulfilment. Judge Bonello's vision is of a State which ceases to serve as the instrument of power of potentates and their entourages. He essentially declaims the fundamental values and principles of the Constitutional State, the Modern State.

This is the message Giovanni Bonello sets to convey: the urgency to apply for membership of, and finally join, Modernity. Leonardo Sciascia once wrote that Modernity had bypassed his native Sicily. The same could be said about Malta. Judge Bonello is campaigning, as it were, for a mentality revolution so profound that Malta would finally embrace Modernity once and for all.

This book is an inverted paean to the Constitutional Court. It implicitly sings praise for the role the Constitutional Court could play if only our democracy were Modern and not dysfunctional. For this reason, *Misunderstanding the Constitution* is not a book only for lawyers, even though lawyers would greatly benefit from reading it. It is instead a book also and mainly for the common citizen desirous of understanding the workings of a democracy that works.

A messy situation but knowledge is power

Judge Bonello wrote a series of 21 articles for another newspaper and these were reworked into the 21 chapters of this book. They take the reader along a journey, each subtly raising questions which the successive chapter answers, usually forcefully. The author's literary prowess is striking, and the underlying structure of the book is nothing short of brilliant because of this concealed concatenation of arguments. During this intellectual journey, one finds a distillation of Judge Bonello's experiences in constitutional (human rights) cases as well as his coruscating criticism of the messy situation prevailing in this country where the understanding and application of the constitutional law are concerned.

For indeed a messy situation it is. At least, this is one of the book's two principal messages I have managed to decipher. The other, however, is a message of hope: knowledge is power. If the citizen (be she a lawyer or not) is aware of her rights and how a proper democracy should function, then the chances of her rights being trampled upon are significantly reduced.

Tears and laughter

The text oozes irony, mockery, and sardonic comment at every punctuation mark. Humour is Judge Bonello's *forte*, and the funnier it is, the harder it hits. But it is not to be classified as "humour" because he is dying to crack jokes. He resorts to humour out of exasperation. As the renowned Danish philosopher mused, "What if everything in the world were a misunderstanding, what if laughter were really tears?"

Judge Bonello's book is a merciless indictment of the judicial organ of the Maltese State and its almost unbelievable inability to understand, appreciate and put into practice the philosophy underlying the provisions of our constitutional instrument, mostly in the domain of human rights. It is a treatise on the philosophy of Maltese human rights law, which uses the technique of appeal to extremes, a technique that necessitates that the conclusion be ridiculous. Hence the "humour" in Judge Bonello's writing.

No wonder Vincent Degaetano, former Chief Justice and current Strasbourg judge for Malta, and Kevin Aquilina, Dean of the Faculty of Laws and one of our topmost legal intellectuals, could not contain their enthusiasm for this gem of a book in their introductory essays.

Whereas Judge Degaetano endorses the book and its main theses, Professor Aquilina's lengthy introductory essay explains, in terms accessible to the layman, the background to the book, its *raison d'être* in the local legal context, and why it is so consequential. Kevin Aquilina is like a reporter reporting from the battlefield where Judge Bonello is busy unleashing his firepower on the enemy.

But who is the enemy?

Giovanni Bonello is the champion of the individual aggrieved twice by a callous State. Twice because the Executive branch tramples upon the person's rights only to be followed by the Judiciary's failure to do anything meaningful about it. For Judge Bonello, the constitution is a social contract and one of its covenants is that the Constitutional Court should serve as its custodian and guarantor, not as defender of the stronger party.

Sovereignty

Judge Bonello chastises judges and other State officials for failing to read and understand the often direct wording of the constitutional instrument, ending up producing perverse results that offend the basic tenets of Democracy. He is mostly angered by the slavish interpretation imposed on the constitutional instrument particularly in the matter of whether the principles established in the case won by one individual against the State should apply only to that individual or to all those who find themselves in the same situation.

We have the absurd situation at the moment that the principles apply only to the party suing the State, and this disturbs Giovanni Bonello no end. One can understand him. And we can equally understand his reaction. He wants to see rationality tame a system which evolved out of historical circumstances.

Let me try to explain.

We Maltese keep mechanically repeating to whoever wants to pay heed – without, I think, a deep understanding of what we are repeating – that our constitutional system follows the Westminster model. In reality, we should be expressing a different notion, namely that we have a Westminster-type constitution. This might seem like a sophism, but it is not.

If we really were to mean that we *follow* the Westminster model, then that would mean that the rules created for and applied to England are the rules that obtain in Malta. On the other hand, if we were to mean that we have a Westminster-type constitution, then it would mean that we interpret our foreign-inspired (as opposed to autochthonous) constitutional instrument in our own way. Ultimately, the constitutional instrument exists within a wider Constitution, which consists of conventions and other unwritten practices, of lower-ranking laws, but more importantly of the history of the people and of the people's world-view and self-perception. Why should we live according to the world-view of the English? Are we English? Are we expected to "ape our betters"?

This is how I understand Judge Bonello's philosophy and I think it is not legal heresy. I will say why.

First, let me quote an expert in the field. Professor Paolo Lacché has argued in *The Journal of Constitutional History* (2017), in an article called "The Sovereignty of the Constitution", that even if the text of a constitutional instrument is copied, the constitution is still original (p. 132). Even if it is *constitutionalisme octroyé* (constitutionalism granted from above), the constitutional document is still the expression of sovereignty. By following blindly the rules of Westminster meant for England, we undermine our own sovereignty.

Secondly, consider the case of our Civil Code as an analogy. In many instances, our Civil Code is a carbon copy of the *Code Napoléon*. Whereas we do refer to French authors, ultimately it is the Maltese judge who interprets the Code, and the Maltese judge is in no way bound to follow the teachings of the French authors on the *Code Napoléon* from which our Civil Code derives. The final word belongs to the Maltese judge. And that is how it should be. We should interpret in our way texts that might have originated from elsewhere.

To put it tautologically, sovereignty means sovereignty.

Erga omnes application

The pertinence of this reasoning to the *erga omnes* debate cannot be overstated.

Let me clarify.

I'm referring to whether the effects of judgments in human rights cases ought to apply only to the parties to the suit (*inter partes*) or to everybody (*erga omnes*). Judge Bonello has decried the current absurdity according to which if a court decision finds that a law is in breach of the human rights provisions of the Constitution, its effects are deemed to benefit only the parties to the suit. Everybody else still risks having their identical rights identically trampled upon. The Constitutional Court thinks it is not empowered to strike the offending law off the statute books (negative law-making), but instead has to wait for Parliament to execute the abrogation at its leisure and convenience (positive law-making in the form of abrogation).

The first sore point here is that this is inspired by English legal theory (itself the product of England's history), which considers Parliament to be supreme. The second sore point is that it is held that Malta should and shall abide by English legal theory.

But this is wrong and Judge Bonello is fully justified to argue otherwise. Whereas he never enters into this particular aspect of the debate, he is justified because the English system and the Maltese system are not identical and the two countries have gone through different historical experiences.

In England, it all started in the 13th century when the English had had enough with the Pope interfering in their internal politics (or that's how they saw it). This was not only the beginning of English anti-Popery. It was also the watershed moment when the English stopped including in their discourse the "Law of Nature", a phrase used by the Church of Rome to refer her children to the higher law they would have broken when they erred.

The void left in the wake of no longer referring to the Law of Nature was filled by the Common Law. In 1610, the great English jurist Edward Coke crystallised the notion that the Common Law was superior to both statute law and custom, and that it was the judge's role to determine what the Common Law said and whether the other two laws conformed to it or not. The judge replaced the Pope, and the Common Law replaced the Law of Nature. Legal historians have even entertained the idea that there was a sort of deification of the Common Law.

But then the Glorious Revolution took place in 1688, and legislative supremacy triumphed in England. The idea that Parliament, and not the Common Law, is supreme is a legacy of Cromwell's dictatorship and the political circumstances of that moment in England's history with which we Maltese have nothing to do.

The same fate did not befall the American Colonies; these continued to follow the tradition that there is a higher law. The American Colonies, however, did deviate from the original model. The parliamentary supremacy brought about by the Glorious Revolution was understood in the Colonies to mean that if a colonial law went against the sovereign will of the English Parliament, then that colonial law would be null and void. In other words, English statute law (law passed by the English Parliament) became for the Colonies what the Common Law (and before it the Law of Nature) had previously been for England.

With the attainment of independence – and this was not limited to America, it happened also in Canada, Australia, India – the new constitutional instruments took the place previously occupied by English statute law. This was how judicial review came to be in America.

Furthermore, the Americans have the *stare decisis* setup, also known as legal precedent, which means that the decisions of a higher court bind a lower court. For the Americans it was therefore natural that no case should have *erga omnes* effects (applicable to all) but that all cases should only have *inter partes* effects (applicable only to the parties). Their *stare decisis* system meant that ultimately decisions of unconstitutionality would be applied to everybody.

Did our local law have a relationship to English law similar to that between American colonial law and English statute law? No, it did not. Do we have the legal precedent setup in Malta? No, we do not: in Malta, court judgments do not bind other courts. Which means that if we want to get out of the current quagmire, we have to follow the continental model (derived from Hans Kelsen's theoretical formulations) and consider constitutional (human rights) cases as having *erga omnes* effects.

This is why, in my view, Judge Bonello is right.

Why this book is the most important book of the decade

Judge Bonello's book belongs to a tradition in which prominent legal figures write polemics meant to enlighten both their legal brethren and the general public. In line with this tradition, the author's ideas are stripped of their legalese garments and exposed in their bareness for all to behold, and understand.

Lord Hewart, Lord Chief Justice of England, did something similar when he penned a powerful but very readable polemic published in 1929, *The New Despotism,* in which he argued that the conferment of discretionary decision-making powers on Ministers (to be exercised, in particular, by officials) undermined the rule of law by opening the door to arbitrariness. (Against Lord Hewart's position one could argue that putting all one's eggs in one basket is myopic. As Lord Shaw of Dunfermline remarked, "To remit the maintenance of constitutional right to the region of judicial discretion is to shift the foundations of freedom from the rock to the sand.")

Which is why Giovanni Bonello's *Misunderstanding the Constitution* is the most important book of the decade. Because the arbitrariness of ministers and their minions and of judges can be contained only by the enlightenment and awareness of the public. This is why Tom Bingham published his (award-winning) *The Rule of Law* in 2010, and the late Stefano Rodotà his *Il diritto di avere diritti* (2013). Because the public needs to know its rights and how the system should work for those rights to be availed of and protected. This is why Giovanni Bonello wrote a book accessible to the general public, bereft of legal verbiage.

Because the general public needs to know that it can sue the State to protect the natural and the historical environment under Chapter II of our constitutional instrument. The staff at the Attorney-General's office needs to know that sometimes it is more consonant with the Constitution to just not argue a case in Strasbourg and leave it to the discretion of the Court. Protesters need to know that the Constitution protects their right to protest and the Police have no right to disallow them. They need to know that the Constitution does not tolerate the authoritarian situation in which the right is first trampled upon and then, perhaps one day many years later, a sort of rickety remedy is found and offered. The citizen needs to know that the

Constitution wants having recourse to the Constitutional Court to be the first line of action and only exceptionally the last resort after all other possible remedies have been exhausted. The man and woman in the street need to know that the Constitution deems their rights sacrosanct and not a privilege or a concession.

The only defect of this book is that possibly its author thinks that everybody is as courageous as he is.

Or perhaps it is an invitation.

Perhaps this is what Giovanni Bonello set out to accomplish: to enlighten the Maltese people. Just like the *philosophes* before him, who enlightened the French. And whoever reads this precious little book, whether he's a lawyer, a lawman, or a layman, he will be enlightened. If all of us see the light, things will have to change and our rights will be taken seriously. If only all of us, every single one of us, were really to understand the Constitution, then nobody would undermine our human rights anymore.

Intriguing aspects of Maltese legal history

Review of
Collected Essays in Maltese Legal History and Comparative Law,
Volume I
by Giuseppe Mifsud Bonnici

The Times of Malta
March 26, 2017

I recently came across this book which, however, had been published in January 2016. And, therefore, this is 'a better-late-than-never' short review.

The book brings under one cover four essays in juridical studies, three of which had already appeared separately in the annual law review *Id-Dritt*, published by the Malta Law Students' Society and one in *Melita Historica*, published by the Malta Historical Society.

The four essays are not thematically connected, so each of them can be treated on its own without reference to the others.

The first essay is titled 'Juridical Importation into Maltese Law of Italian Private Law solutions and its implications' (*Id-Dritt*, Vol. 25, 2015). This 'importation' of a foreign element into our legal system is quite a common jurisprudential practice by our courts which, given the similarity of many of our institutes of law to those present in Italian civil law, is a salutary and enriching practice.

But, of course, there also lies an obvious trap for the insufficiently attentive judge who, following this practice in a rather blind and haphazard way, applies what he considers to be Italian law, theory and practice.

When Maltese law on the matter is completely different from the Italian one such a judge would not only deliver a grave misinterpretation of Maltese law but even worse, would commit a serious injustice by not applying in the matter before him the right law and its solution of the relevant rights and obligations.

The author does not give examples of what he is rightly lamenting, but perhaps one could point out as an outstanding case in point the application of Italian rules that are not compatible with Maltese law which in the institute of spoliation – [*spoll*] does not allow any plea by the defendant except that which is relevant as to the facts regarding the possession or detention and of the spoliation acts themselves [Art. 791 {3} of the Code of Organisation and Civil Procedure].

And yet, certain judgments of Maltese courts have allowed pleas based on the intention of the person who has committed the spoliation and got away with it.

The author points out the further problem that some Maltese judges did not pay sufficient attention to the fact that looking at Italian law based on the code of 1865, which is quite similar to Malta's, not noticing that the Italian code of 1942 is quite different in many respects.

It has been mythified that the British liberal spirit infiltrated the Maltese legal system

The second essay is titled 'Historical Facts and Myths surrounding the Criminal Code of Malta', which had originally appeared in *Id-Dritt*, Vol. 22, 2012. It is a study of the genesis of our Criminal Law Code.

The beginning is traced back to 1831 when a commission was appointed by the Colonial Administration, chaired by Chief Justice Sir John Stoddart, with a Maltese judge and three Englishmen, charged with compiling a Criminal Law Code.

This commission was dissolved and replaced by another in 1834 which this time, however, more sensibly was composed of four Maltese judges and a Maltese jurist. They drew up two codes – the Criminal Law one, and accompanied it by another dealing with Criminal Procedure. They did this in 1835.

The Secretary of State, however, requested the commissioners to review once again what they had done, and the revised project was ready by 1842, together with an explanatory report.

At this point, the Secretary of State appointed Andrew Jameson, a Scottish lawyer, to look at the proposed code and to make any observations he deemed fit.

During my student studies at the University of Malta, Jameson was not only appreciated for his comments on the draft Criminal Codes drawn up by Maltese jurists – four judges and a lawyer – but was almost granted the honour of having compiled the whole code himself. It is then that the author identifies Jameson as the person around whose image some Maltese jurists have created certain myths.

It has been mythified that the British liberal spirit infiltrated the Maltese legal system. The author blames Jameson as being the source of this boastful assertion, which he cannot accept, as it is incompatible with the man who was so much in favour of capital punishment and who expressed the thought that he was afraid that the Maltese – as people of the south – would dilute certain punishments in the code to lessen their severity.

The essay is quite an interesting contribution to the history of Maltese legislation.

The third essay is titled 'Medieval [Legal] beasts in our midst'. Co-authored with Patrick Cuignet, the essay is, in fact, a study in Comparative Law. It examines in detail the legal terms *résiliation, resiliment* and *résolution* with reference to contracts.

The use of one or more of these terms, beginning with the Code Napoleon and through the Codes of the State of Louisiana, that of Quebec, the Kingdom of the Two Sicilies, the Italian Code, and ending up with the Maltese Civil Code, extending it to the different uses of the two terms in our jurisprudence, and ending up in a *Post Scriptum* which notes that the Maltese unit of the European Court of Justice is now translating *résiliation* as *xoljiment* and *résolution* as *ħall*.

The author keeps his distance from this practice, remarking that the terms in our law are, in fact, used synonymously.

The last essay is an analysis of what the author himself says is of an obscure term – *midheb* – which he found in Vassalli's *Lexicon*. He describes his finding in the title of the essay 'Latin wine decanted into a Semitic carafe'. So this essay is more of a linguistic journey with a faint legal connection. Like father, like son.

The author's father was Frans Sammut, a linguist and novelist of repute, which explains the author's curiosity in researching such an archaic term that is unknown to the great majority of Maltese speakers, including myself.

In his quest to explain the very existence of the term which appears only in Vassalli, the author carries out a veritable insightful examination of Arab and even Jewish languages and legal structures, but in the end he seems to come to the regretful conclusion that this word, like others of the same type, such as *baqgħa*, never formed part of our legal terminology.

The writer is a first-class researcher, ranging far and wide and following all the trails, primary and secondary, which that research suggests. This is quite impressive.

Bibliography

Books and Chapters in Books

The Appeals of the Nobility and People of Malta, to the Justice, Public Faith, and Policy, of the British Government, for the Fulfilment of the conditions upon which they gave up their Island to the King, namely, their Ancient Rights, under a Free Constitution, London: Henry Reynell, 1811

ANON., *Important Notices of Malta and Gozo*, Malta: Anglo-Maltese Printing Press, 1846

ANON.: *Annotazioni alle Leggi Criminali per l'Isola di Malta e Sue Dipendenza da Servire di Guida al Giurato per cura d'un giovane Avvocato maltese*, Malta: Tipo-Litografia Anglo-Maltese, 1870

ANON.: *Common Consent, The Basis of the Constitution of England; or, Parliamentary Reform, Considered and Tried by the Tests of Law and Reason*, London: Allman, 1817

ASCHERI, Mario: 'Grandi Tribunali Italiani d'età moderna' in *Il contributo italiano alla storia del pensiero – Diritto, Enciclopedia Italiana*, 2012

AZOPARDI, Baron: *Raccolta di Varie Cose Antiche e Moderne Utili ed Interessanti Riguardanti Malta e Gozo*, Malta, 1843

BAXI, U.: 'Postcolonial Legacy' in *A Companion to Postcolonial Studies*, H. Schwarz & S. Ray (eds.), Oxford: Blackwell, 2000, 540–555

BECCARIA, Cesare: *On Crimes and Punishments* (David Young tr), Indianapolis: Hackett Publishing 1986 [1764]

BELTON, J.: *The English Masonic Union of 1813: A Tale Antient and Modern*, Bury St Edmonds, Suffolk: Arima Publishing, 2012

BOGDAN, H., & Snoek, J.A.M.: 'The History of Freemasonry: An Overview', in Bogdan, H., & Snoek, J.A.M. (ed.), *Handbook of Freemasonry*, Leiden/Boston: Brill, 2014, 13–32

BONELLO, Giovanni: 'For a History of Lawyering in Malta' in Giovanni Bonello, *Histories of Malta: Deceptions and Perceptions*, Vol 1, Malta: Fondazzjoni Patrimonju Malti, 2000

-----------------------: *Misunderstanding the Constitution: How the Maltese judiciary undermines human rights*, Malta: BDL, 2018

BRIGANTI, Tommaso: *Pratica Criminale*, Vol 2, Naples: Gabriele Marotta Libraio Editore 1842 [1755]

CADOPPI, Alberto: *Materiali per un'introduzione allo studio del Diritto Penale Comparato*, Padua: CEDAM, 2001

CARBASSE, Jean-Marie: *Introduction historique au droit penal*, Paris: PUF, 1990

---------------------------: 'État autoritaire et justice répressive. L'évolution de la législation penale de 1789 au Code Pénal de 1810' in *All'Ombra dell'Aquila Imperiale. Trasformazioni e continuità istituzionali nei territori sabaudi in età napoleonica (1802-1814). Atti del Convegno, Torino 15-18 ottobre 1990*, vol I, Rome: Ministero per i beni culturali e ambientali, 1994

CARCERERI DE PRATI, Claudio: 'Introduzione: Le riforme giudiziarie a Malta nella second metà del XVIII secolo' in Nicola Picardi & Alessandro Giuliani (eds), *Codice di Malta 1777/1784*, Milan: Giuffrè, 2001

CARONI, Pio: *Saggi sulla storia della codificazione*, Milan: Giuffrè, 1998

CASSOLA, Arnold: *The Literature of Malta: An Example of Unity in Diversity*, Malta: Minima Publishing, 2000

CATTANEO, Mario Alessandro: 'Un codice penale post-illuminista' in Sergio Vinciguerra (ed), *Codice Penale degli Stati Uniti delle Isole Jonie (1841)*, Padua: CEDAM, 2008

CESARINI, Antonella: *Una rivoluzione in forma di legge: Malta 1974 storia di una anomala revisione costituzionale*, Padua: CEDAM, 2001

CHIANTINI, Monica: 'Diritto e processo penale alla fine dell'*Ancien Régime*' in Mario Ascheri (ed), *Lezioni di storia della codificazione e delle costituzioni*, Turin: Giappichelli, 2008

CIAPPARA, Frans: *Enlightenment and Reform in Malta 1740- 1798*, Malta: Midsea Books, 2006

--------------------: *Church-State Relations in Late-Eighteenth-Century Malta*, Malta: Malta University Press, 2018

COBURN, K. (ed.): *The Notebooks of Samuel Taylor Coleridge Vol. 3: 1808-1819 Notes*, Abingdon: Routledge, 2002 [1973]

COLAO, Floriana: *La giustizia criminale senese nell'età delle riforme leopoldine: post tenebras spero lucem*, Milan: Giuffrè, 1989

-------------------: 'Il codice di Malta in un «articolo» di Mittermaier per «La Temi» e l'*Avvertenza* di Giuseppe Panattoni' in Sergio Vinciguerra (ed), *Leggi Criminali per l'Isola di Malta e Sue Dipendenze (1854)*, Padua: CEDAM, 2003

COLLEY, Linda: *Acts of Union and Disunion: What has held the UK together and what has divided it?*, London: Profile Books, 2014

Creasy, Sir Edward: *The Imperial and Colonial Constitutions of the Britannic Empire*, London: Longmans, Green, and Co., 1872

Cremona, J.J.: *The Maltese Constitution and Constitutional History since 1813* (Malta: PEG, 1994)

----------------: *The Maltese Constitution and Constitutional History Since 1813* (2nd ed.), PEG, Malta, 1997

Da Passano, Mario: 'La codificazione del diritto penale a Napoli nel periodo francese' in Sergio Vinciguerra (ed), *Le Leggi Penali di Giuseppe Bonaparte per il Regno di Napoli (1808)*, Padua: CEDAM, 1996

-----------------------: 'Le *Leggi Penali* Napoletane e il Primo Progetto di Codice Penale Maltese (1836)' in Sergio Vinciguerra (ed), *Leggi Criminali per l'Isola di Malta e Sue Dipendenza (1854)*, Padua: CEDAM, 2003

De Caro, L.: *Il Processo Criminale in Malta*, Malta: Tipografia Sda Vescovo, 1845

De Pascale, Carla: 'Romagnosi, Gian Domenico' in A. Clericuzio, S. Ricci (eds.), *Il contributo italiano alla storia del Pensiero – Filosofia*, Istituto della Enciclopedia Italiano, 2012 (online edition)

de Smith, S.A.: *The New Commonwealth and its Constitutions*, London: Stevens & Sons, 1964

Dezza, Ettore: '"Per li tempi d'avvenire siano abolite le torture". Note sulla disciplina del processo penale nel Codice Municipale di Malta del 1784' in Ettore Dezza (ed), *Saggi di Storia del Processo Penale nell'Età della Codificazione*, Padua: CEDAM 2001

----------------: '"La corte vi domanda se siete reo o innocente". Istituti di *Common Law* nel codice di procedura penale degli Stati Uniti delle Isole Jonie (1844)' in Sergio Vinciguerra (ed), *Codice Penale degli Stati Uniti delle Isole Jonie (1841)*, Padua: CEDAM, 2008

Dillon, John Joseph: *A Memoir concerning the Political State of Malta*, London: Booker, 1807

------------------------: *The Letters of Hibern-Anglus, containing Strictures on the conduct of the Present Administration in Ireland, and a Vindication of the Proceedings adopted since the Regency by the Irish Catholics, With Other Papers*, London: Ridgway, and Booker, 1811

Edigati, Daniele: *Prima della "Leopoldina": la giustizia criminale toscana tra prassi e riforme legislative nel XVIII secolo*, Naples: Jovene, 2011

Feola, Raffaele: *Dall'Illuminismo alla Restaurazione: Donato Tommasi e la legislazione delle Sicilie*, Naples: Jovene, 1977

Ferrante, Riccardo: '"Padroni dell'uso de' capitali senza le leggi proibitive degli altri governi". Diritto penale ed economia nelle Isole Ionie' in Sergio Vinciguerra (ed), *Codice Penale degli Stati Uniti delle Isole Jonie (1841)*, Padua: CEDAM, 2008

Ganado, Albert: *La storia del codice penale di Malta del 1854. Un breve ragguaglio* in Sergio Vinciguerra (ed), *Leggi Criminali per l'Isola di Malta e Sue Dipendenze (1854)*, Padua: CEDAM, 2003

Gandinus, Albertus: *Tractatus de maleficiis*, Vols 1 & 2, Berlin: Walter de Gruyter, 1926 [1460]

Garbagnati, Giovanni & Lupária, Luca: 'Il processo penale maltese tra modello *adversary* e radici continentali' in Lorenzo Cuocolo & Luca Lupária (eds), *Valori costituzionali e nuove politiche del diritto. Scritti raccolti in occasione del decennale della rivista 'Cahiers Européens'*, Matelica: Halley Editrice, 2007

Garré, Roy: 'The Dynamics of Law Formation in Italian Legal Science during the Early Modern Period: the Function of Custom' in Wim Blockmans, André Holenstein, & Jon Mathieu (eds), *Empowering Interactions: Political Cultures and the Emergence of the State in Europe 1300-1900*, Surrey: Ashgate, 2009

Gekas, Sakis: *Xenocracy: State, Class and Colonialism in the Ionian Islands, 1815-1864*, Oxford: Berghahn, 2017

Gourlay, Douglas: *Sheriff Andrew Jameson: The Life of Effie Gray's Uncle*, Ely, Cambs: Melrose Books, 2015

Harding, Hugh W.: *Maltese Legal History Under British Rule (1801-1836)*, Malta: self-published, 1968

Hardman, William: *A History of Malta during the Period of the French and British Occupations 1798–1815* Part II, London: Longmans, 1909

Hawes, James: *The Shortest History of England*,Exeter: Old Street Publishing, 2021

Hone, William: *Buonapartephobia: The Origin of Dr. Slop's Name*, London, 1820

Hough, Barry & Davis, Howard: 'The British Claim to Rule Malta 1800–1813' in Lee, H., Hough, B., & Davis, H., *Constitutional History of Malta 1800-1914*, Oxford: Oxford Legal Publishing, 2017

Ince, Onur Ulas: *Colonial Capitalism and the Dilemmas of Liberalism*, Oxford: Oxford University Press, 2020

Jameson, Andrew: *Report on the Proposed Code of Criminal Laws for the Island of Malta and its Dependencies*, Malta, 1844

Jennings, Ivor: *The British Constitution*, Cambridge: Cambridge University Press, 1966 (5th ed.)

Kirkby, Coel: 'The Making of Empire', in Peter Cane & Harshan Kumarasingham (eds), *The Cambridge Constitutional History of the United Kingdom: The Changing Constitution* (Cambridge: Cambridgge University Press, 2023

La Rosa, Giorgio: *Il sigillo delle riforme: la Costituzione di Pietro Leopoldo di Toscana*, Milan: Vita e Pensiero, 1997

Lawson, F.H.: *Many Laws*, Amsterdam: North-Holland Publishing Company, 1977

Lee, Hilde I.: *Malta 1813–1914: A Study in Constitutional and Strategic Development*, Malta: Progress Press, 1972

Lieberman, David: *The Challenge of Codification in English Legal History*, Tokyo: Research Institute of Economy, Trade and Industry, 2009

Listri, P Francesco: *Pietro Leopoldo: Granduca di Toscana, un riformatore del Settecento*, Florence: Leonardo, 2016

Losurdo, Domenico: *Liberalism: A Counter-History* (Gregory Elliott, tr.), London: Verso, 2011

Loughlin, Martin: *Public Law and Political Theory*, Oxford: Clarendon Press, 1992

Mallia-Milanes, Victor: 'The Genesis of Maltese Nationalism' in Victor Mallia-Milanes (ed), *The British Colonial Experience 1800-1964: The Impact on Maltese Society*, Malta: Mireva, 1988

------------------------------: 'Valletta: Malta's Hospitaller City. An Epitome of Europe' in Victor Mallia-Milanes, *Valletta: Malta's Hospitaller City and Other Essays*, Malta: Midsea Books, 2019

Masferrer, Aniceto: 'Tradition and Foreign Influences in the 19th Century Codification of Criminal Law: Dispelling the Myth of the Pervasive

MATTOLINI, Mario: *Il principe illuminato Pietro Leopoldo: la Toscana dei Lorena*, Florence: Medicea, 1981

MAURANO, Silvio: *La repubblica partenopea*, Milan: Ceschina, 1971

MERCIECA, Arturo: *The Making and Unmaking of a Maltese Chief Justice*, Malta: Giov. Muscat, 1969

MICALLEF, Antonio: *Lectures on the Statutes of the Sacred Order of St. John of Jerusalem at the University of Malta 1792* (tr. Michael Galea), Karlsruhe: KIT Scientific Publishing, 2012

MITROVICH, Giorgio: *The Cause of the People of Malta; Now Before Parliament*, London: Effingham Wilson, 1836

MONTESQUIEU: *De l'esprit des lois* (V Goldschmidt, ed.), Paris: Flammarion, 2008

MUSCAT, Niccolò: *Apologia a Favore dell'Inclita Nazione Maltese*, Malta, 1783

OLIVER, G. (1867) *The Origin of the Royal Arch Order of Masonry Historically Considered*, London: Spencer

PENNINGTON, Kenneth: 'The Jurisprudence of Procedure' in Wilfrid Hartmann & Kenneth Pennington (eds.), *The History of Courts and Procedure in Medieval Canon Law*, Washington, DC: The Catholic University of America Press, 2016

PISANI, Gaetano: *Lettera di un maltese ad un Cavaliere Gerosolomitano Professo su i Cinque Ragionamenti del Cavalier Giandonato Rogadeo*, Vercelli, 1783

REFALO, Michael: *The Maltese Nineteenth-Century Notary and His Archives*, Malta: BDL, 2014

RAPINET, G.: *Lectures on the British Constitution and on the Government of Malta*, Malta: A. Aquilina, 1883

ROBERTSON, John: *The Case for The Enlightenment: Scotland and Naples 1680-1760*, Cambridge: Cambridge University Press, 2005

ROGADEO, Gian Donato: *Ragionamenti del Cavaliere Giandonato Rogadeo sul Regolamento della Giustizia, e sulle Pene*, Naples, 1783

ROMAGNANI, Gian Paolo: 'Romagnosi, Giovanni Domenico' in *Dizionario Biografico degli Italiani* Vol. 88, Rome: Treccani, 2017

ROMAGNOSI, Gian Domenico: *Introduzione alla Studio del Diritto Pubblico Universale* in *Scritti sul Diritto Filosofico di G.D. Romagnosi, riordinati ed illustrati da Alessandro de Giorgi*, Palermo: Frascona-Barbera, 1814

ROOKE, Barbara E. (ed.): *The Collected Works of Samuel Taylor Coleridge: The Friend*, Vol 4: II, London-Princeton NJ: Routledge & Kegan Paul Ltd, 1969)

ROSSELLI, John: *Lord William Bentinck and the British Occupation of Sicily 1811-1814*, Cambridge: Cambridge University Press, 1956

------------------: *Lord William Bentinck: The making of a Liberal Imperialist*, Brighton: Sussex University Press, 1974

RUMBLE, Wilfrid E.: *Doing Austin Justice: The Reception of John Austin's Philosophy of Law in Nineteenth-Century England*, London: Continuum, 2005

SALIBA, Paul: *A Manual for Legal Procurators*, Malta: PEG, 1996

SAMMUT, Mark A.: 'Judicial Importation into Maltese Law of Italian Private Law: Solutions and Its Implications' in Mark A. Sammut, *Essays in Maltese Legal History and Comparative Law* Vol. 1, Oxford: OLP, 2017

----------------------: 'Historical Facts and Myths surrounding the Criminal Code of Malta' in Mark A. Sammut, *Essays in Maltese Legal History and Comparative Law* Vol. 1, Oxford: OLP, 2017

SAVELLI, Rodolfo: 'Tribunali, "decisiones" e giuristi: una proposta di ritorno alle fonti' in Giorgio Chittolini, Anthony Molho, & Pierangelo Schiera (eds), *Origini dello Stato. Processi di formazione statale in Italia fra medioevo ed età moderna*, Bologna: il Mulino, 1994

SBRICCOLI, Mario & BETTONI, Antonella (eds), *Grandi tribunali e rote nell'Italia di Antico Regime*, Milan: Giuffré, 1993

SCHIAVONE, Mario (ed.), *Dictionary of Maltese Biographies*, Malta: PIN, 2009

SHORE, Cris: 'The Crown as Metonym for the State?: The Human Face of Leviathan', in C. Shore & D. Williams (eds.), *The Shapeshifting Crown: Locating the State in Postcolonial New Zealand, Australia, Canada and the UK*, Cambridge: Cambridge University Press, 2019

SPIRITO, Ugo: *Storia del diritto penale italiano: da Cesare Beccaria ai nostri giorni*, Milan: Sansoni, 1974

STILE, Alfonso: 'Il codice penale del 1819 per lo Regno delle due Sicilie' in Sergio Vinciguerra, *I Codici Preunitari e il Codice Zanardelli*, Padua: CEDAM, 1993

TARELLO, Giovanni: *Storia della cultura giuridica moderna. Assolutismo e codificazione del diritto*, Bologna: il Mulino, 1976

TOMMASEO-BELLINI, *Nuovo Dizionario della Lingua Italiana*, Vol 3, Part 1, Turin: UTET, 1869

VAN CAENEGEM, Raoul: 'Criminal Law in England and Flanders under King Henry II and Count Philip of Alsace' in RC van Caenegem (ed), *Legal History: A European Perspective*, London: The Hambledon Press, 1991

VAN CAENEGEM, Raoul: *I sistemi giuridici europei* (Emmanuela Bertucci tr), Bologna: il Mulino, 2003

VASSALLI FORMOSE DE FREMAUX, M.A.: *Suggestions in Accordance with Mr. Amabile Bonello's Project of Emigration in the Coasts of North Africa*, Malta, 1867

VELLA, Mario: *Reflections in a Canvas Bag: Beginning philosophy between politics and history*, Malta: PEG, 1989

VINCIGUERRA, Sergio: 'Una tecnica giuridica raffinata per l'assolutismo regio' in Sergio Vinguerra & Mario Da Passano (eds), *Codice per lo Regno delle Due Sicilie (1819), Parte Seconda: Le Leggi Penali*, Padua: CEDAM, 1994

-------------------------: 'Una penalistica italiana al servizio della politica francese: le leggi penali di Giuseppe Bonaparte per il Regno di Napoli (1808)' in Sergio Vinciguerra (ed), *Le Leggi Penali di Giuseppe Bonaparte per il Regno di Napoli (1808)*, Padua: CEDAM, 1996

-------------------------: *Diritto penale italiano: Concetto, fonti, validità, interpretazione*, Vol 1, Padua: CEDAM, 1999

-------------------------: 'Umanità delle pene detentive, prevenzione del reato e ristoro del danno' in Sergio Vinciguerra (ed), *Codice Penale degli Stati Uniti delle Isole Jonie (1841)*, Padua: CEDAM, 2008

VIORA, Mario E: *Consolidazioni e Codificazioni: Contributo alla storia della codificazione*, Turin: Giappichelli, 1967 (3rd edn.)

VORMBAUM, Thomas & BOHLANDER, Michael: *A Modern History of German Criminal Law*, Berlin: Springer-Verlag, 2014

WANDRUSZKA, Adam: *Pietro Leopoldo, un grande riformatore*, Florence: Vallecchi, 1968

WARD, John Manning: *Colonial Self-Government: The British Experience 1759-1856*, London: Macmillan, 1976

WHEARE, K.C.: *Modern Constitutions*, Oxford: Oxford University Press, 1966

Wright, D. (rev.): *Gould's History Of Freemasonry Throughout The World*, Vol. 3, New York: Charles Scribner's Sons, 1936

Zangwill, Israel: *The Principle of Nationalities*, London: Watts & Company, 1917

Zanou, Konstantina: *Transnational Patriotism in the Mediterranean, 1800-1850*, Oxford: Oxford University Press, 2018

Zuliani, Dario: *La riforma penale di Pietro Leopoldo. Presentazione storica e indice delle edizioni della Legge toscana del 30 novembre 1786*, Milan: Giuffrè, 1995

Articles

Agrimi, Mario: 'Antonio Genovesi e l'Illuminismo riformatore nel Mezzogiorno' *Belfagor* 22 (1967) 4

Bonello, Giovanni: 'A Mild Debunking of Dr Gio Nicolò Muscat', *Melita Historica* XVII (2016)

Clark, David: 'Cautious Constitutionalism: Commonwealth Legislative Independence and the Statute of Westminster 1931-1942', *Macquarie Law Journal* 4 (2016) 16

Cobbett, P.: 'The Crown as Representing the State', *Commonwealth Law Review* 1 (1904) 4

Coffey, Donal K.: "Constitutional law and empire in interwar Britain: universities, liberty, nationality and parliamentary supremacy", *Northern Ireland Legal Quarterly* 71 (2020) 2

Conklin, C. N.: 'The Origins of the Pursuit of Happiness', *Washington University Jurisprudence Review*, 7 (2015) 195

Cox, Noel: 'The Theory of Sovereignty and the Importance of the Crown in the Realms of the Queen', *Oxford University Commonwealth Law Journal*, 2 (2002) 2

Deák, Francis, [Review] "*The British Constitution* by W. Ivor Jennings, Cambridge: Cambridge University Press, 1941", *The University of Chicago Law Review*, 9 (1942) 2

DEMETRA, Fr Sorvatzioti & MANSON, Allan: 'Burden of Proof and *L'intime conviction*: Is the Continental Criminal Trial Moving to the Common Law?' *Canadian Criminal Law Review* 23 (2019)

FACINEROSO, Alessia: 'The Sicilian Revolution of 1848 as seen from Malta', *Symposia Melitensia* 6 (2010)

GORLA, Gino: 'I "grandi Tribunali" italiani fra i secoli XVI e XIX: un capitolo incompiuto nella storia politico-giuridica d'Italia', *Quaderni del Foro italiano* 92 (1969)

GOURLAY, Douglas: 'Andrew Jameson and the Origins of the Criminal Code of Malta', *Melita Historica* 15 (2009) 2

HARDING, A.: 'The Westminster Model Constitution Overseas', *Oxford University Commonwealth Law Journal*, 4 (2004) 2

JENNINGS, Ivor: 'A plea for utilitarianism', *Modern Law Review*, 2 (1938) 22

KUMARASINGHAM, H.: 'Sir Ivor Jennings' "The Conversion of History into Law"', *American Journal of Legal History*, 56 (2016)

MALAGODI, Mara: 'Ivor Jennings' Constitutional Legacy beyond the Occidental-Oriental Divide', *Journal of Law and Society*, 42 (2015) 1

MASFERRER, Aniceto: 'Codification as Nationalisation or Denationalisation of Law: The Spanish Case in Comparative Perspective', *Comparative Legal History* 4 (2016)

--------------------------: 'French Codification and 'Codiphobia' in Common Law Traditions', *The Tulane European and Civil Law Forum*, 34 (2019)

MITTERMAIER, Carl: 'Il Codice Maltese sulle contravvenzioni, e le leggi e regolamenti di Polizia con notizie sulla redazione del Codice Criminale di Malta', *La Temi: Giornale di Legislazione e di Giurisprudenza* 4 (1853)

NORTH, Peter M.: 'Problems of Codification in a Common Law System', *Rabels Zeitschrift für ausländisches und internationales Privatrecht / The Rabel Journal of Comparative and International Private Law*, 3 (1982)

O'RAHILLY, Alfred, 'Allegiance and the Crown', *An Irish Quarterly Review,* 11 (1922) 42

ORLANDI, Giuseppe: 'Il Regno di Napoli nel Settecento', *Spicilegium Historicum Congregationis SSmi Redemptoris* 44 (1996) 1

PARLATO, Vittorio: 'Pietro Leopoldo: Un Principe Riformatore', *Studi urbinati, scienze giuridiche, politiche ed economiche* 67 (2016) 3–4

POSTEMA, Gerard J.: 'Classical Common Law Jurisprudence (Part II)', *Oxford University Commonwealth Law Journal,* Summer 2003

READ, James R: 'The New Constitution of Nigeria, 1979: "The Washington Model"?', *Journal of African Law,* 23 (1979) 2

SAUNDERS, Cheryl: 'The Concept of the Crown', *Melbourne University Law Review,* 38 (2015)

SCHWARTZ, LB: 'The Collection of European Penal Codes and the Study of Comparative Law', *University of Pennsylvania Law Review* 106 (1958) 3

STANTON, John: 'The Constitution of Malta: Supremacy, Parliament and Separation of Powers', *Journal of International and Comparative Law,* 6 (2019) I

TUR, R.H.S.: 'What is Jurisprudence?', *The Philosophical Quarterly* 28 (1978)

WILSON, Jon & DILLEY, Andrew: 'The Incoherence of Empire, Or, the Pitfalls of Ignoring Sovereignty in the History of the British Empire', *Transactions of the Royal Historical Society* 1 (2023)

XUEREB, Charles: 'Malta Stockholm Syndrome (or why we love the British)', 13 *THINK Magazine* (2015), 48–55

Others

Avvertimenti, Collezione di Bandi, Prammatiche ed Altri Avvisi Ufficiali pubblicati dal Governo dell'Isola di Malta e Sue Dipendenze dal 17 Luglio 1784, al 4 Ottobre 1813

Cenni Biografici in Memoria dell'Amico e Patriota Amabile Bonello, Tipografia del *Risorgimento,* Malta, 1879

Cobbett's Annual Register, Vol. III, from January to June 1803, London: Cox and Baylis, July 1803

Encyclopœdia Britannica, 1911 edition, s.v. 'British Empire'

Hansard's Parliamentary Debates Third Series, 2° Victoriæ, 1839 6 (1839)

Rapporto dei Commissarj di Sua Maestà per la formazione di Nuovi Codici di Legge, per l'Isola di Malta e sue Dipendenze, sui due Progetti, l'uno di Leggi Penali, e l'altro di Leggi di Organizzazione e Procedura Penale, Malta, 1835

Report respecting the Courts and the Administration of the Law at Malta; made by Sir John Richardson Knight His Majesty's Commissioner, 19 August 1826, National Archives of Malta GMR 4

The Critical Review. Or, Annals of Literature Series theThird, Vol. XI, London: J. Mawman, 1807

The Monthly Review, or Literary Journal of England Vol. LIV, London: Becket, 1807

Vocabolario dell'Accademia della Crusca Vol, 3 (4th edn) 1729-1738

Vocabolario Italiano e Latino, Padua, 1770

* * *

Bonello, Giovanni: 'Notes for a History of the Judiciary at the time of the Order' [2007] https://judiciary.mt/en/Documents/PDF/A%20History%20of%20the%20Judiciary.pdf, accessed 15 October 2021

Eleanya, Sam: *Nigeria: Constitutional Development and History* https://constitution.lawnigeria.com/2018/03/26/nigeria-constitution-development-and-history/ (accessed 1 November 2023)

* * *

Ganado, Albert: [undated] 'Sir John Stoddart (1773-1856)' https://judiciary.mt/en/Documents/bio/Sir%20John%20Stoddart.pdf, accessed 15 October 2021

Ndulo, Muna: 'Constitutions and Constitutional Reforms in African Politics', https://oxfordre.com/politics/display/10.1093/acrefore/9780190228637.001.0001/acrefore-9780190228637-e-1324 (accessed 1 November 2023)

Formosa, Daniela: 'The 1836 Austin and Lewis Commission: An Analytical Review of Private Correspondences and Reports' (unpublished BA thesis) University of Malta, 2017

* * *

"Sylvanus Urban": 'Sir John Joseph Dillon', *The Gentleman's Magazine*, Vol. III, July to December 1837, London: Pickering

* * *

Mifsud Bonnici, Giuseppe: 'The Supremacy of Parliament', *The Times of Malta*, 2 June 2012

Vassallo, Carmel, 'A nationless state or a stateless nation', *The Times of Malta*, 9 February 2003

Index of Names

K

L

M

N

W

X

Z

Notes

Notes

Printed by BoD™in Norderstedt, Germany